# SATURN

## Redrawing the Outlines of Our Lives

*Rev. Alice Miller, LMAFA*

ISBN-13: 978-0-86690-675-3

Cover Design: Jack Cipolla

Published by:
American Federation of Astrologers, Inc.
6535 S. Rural Road
Tempe, AZ 85283

www.astrologers.com

# From the Author

The writing of this book began under a Saturn transit conjunction my second house Moon. It concludes with Saturn trine my Sun from my tenth house.

There are many Saturn books on the market. I have integrated elements learned from many other writers into this work, interweaving their themes with my own perspectives. I owe much to writers like Dane Rudhyar, Liz Greene, and Marc Robertson, who have helped me to weather many Saturn transits, including two returns. In this book, I wish to honor them, not replace them. Like all of my work, it is a synthesis of astrological, metaphysical, and psychological thought. And, as always, I shall attempt to write in modern American English, avoiding unclear esoteric terms. In doing so, I hope to show readers some previously unrecognized faces of Saturn, to make him your friend, or at the least, not your enemy. He was never a devil, never Satan. He was only a line that we drew around our lives. His location in our chart defined the place beyond which we were taught that it was not safe to go. He anchored us to the past and kept us grounded in reality.

Rev. Alice Miller's Web site

www.lifeprintastrology.com


Rev. Alice Miller's Publications

Principles of Astrology: Planets, Signs & Houses

Dynamics of Astrology: Interpreting Aspects

The Soul of Astrology: Inner Dimensions of the Modern Moon

Retrograde Planets and Consciousness

Healing the Inner Child: The Astrology of Family Dysfunction

Getting Birth Charts On Target: LMT, Turning, Adoptions


Designs for a New Age: The Grand Cross: Rectangles and Yods

Interceptions: Heralds of a New Age

Intercepted Planets: Possibilities for a New Age

Pagan Astrology for Soul and Spirit

From the Nodes to Fortuna: Journey and Goal

Astrology's Tree of Life

*In Memoriam*

Thank you and Good-Bye to

The Corona Light Group

1955-2000

its Hostess, Fern Fair Pickering, and

its long-time Teacher, Garth Gebhart both of whom departed this Earth in 2005


You came to grow, to expand the light

Your mission now is,

To relight the stars from which you came.

# Foreword

Human consciousness is forever on the rise, reaching for something more, something better. It is a cyclic growth process, proceeding step by step. Each step has its own parameters. As physical growth has phases, so does spiritual growth.

The intra-uterine or non-visible stages are the first, second, and third trimesters of pregnancy. These represent conception, embodiment, and consciousness. They also represent spiritual quickening, physical formation, and the breath of awareness.

Next comes birth. We enter the world, becoming visible to all. After that comes childhood, adolescence, young adulthood, the productive years, middle-age, and retirement. Beyond that are two final phases which we call galactic and cosmic. Their evolutionary correlation is symbolized by the twelve astrological signs.

Each phase has its outline or boundary. The first three signs are limited by the maternal womb. It must be viable for quickening. It must be sufficiently developed and healthy for the growth of the fetus. In the final sign, the child is making itself known to its mother. Her attention, her attitude, her state of mind, all set the stage for the later individuation of her child.

The limits of infancy clearly belong to the mother (and/or other caretakers). She defines its horizons. Initially, they may be a crib, a playpen. As the child learns to crawl, limits may be extended to a room or the entire house. Once the child learns to walk, those limits may extend to a yard, if the mother has one available. Other limits are those of being required to hold adult hands or stay within their sight.

As we move into the childhood stage, entering school, our limits expand again. Now we may be allowed to walk to school, first with accompaniment, then alone, or to ride a school bus. We begin to be allowed to visit friends unaccompanied by an adult. Often we are allowed to spend a night, even a few days, away from parents.

Adolescence becomes a proving ground for Saturn. Rules become a big issue when the behavior of the individual swings between childish and mature. Simultaneously, parents may be dealing with the beginning of separation anxiety. It is also a time when offspring begin to challenge their authority figures. Maturity brings certain rights. Parents and children must work out the schedule for the transition from childhood to adulthood, adapting rules and expanding rights accordingly. The first Saturn opposition around age 14-15 often brings a crisis point for this period.

Then comes young adulthood and emancipation, often marked by the first Uranus square near age 21. This can vary, depending on when the educational process ends. Until then, parents usually retain some control, some authority, from their financial contributions.

Ordinarily both end as offspring begin careers and/or their own families. This period officially extends to the first Saturn return near age thirty.

Ordinarily, we are officially emancipated before age thirty. The Saturn return is the designated time for leaving behind the last parental limits. At this time we claim the right to set our own rules for how we will live–including whether and how we will rear a family. Until then, though on our own, we tend to continue following parental patterns and examples.

The first Saturn return is about claiming our full rights to live as we choose, and by our own authority. From here on, the rules are ours to make. Some Saturns know this much bettter than others. Some individuals will spend years escaping their childhood conditioning. Many are working on this phase of individuation up to the Uranus opposition in or near the early forties. We thus review our lives, examining what we have accomplished and how we feel about it.

At that point, if we have not done so, events may do it for us. How we have dealt with Saturn issues between ages 21 and 40 determines the stress level of the mid-life crisis.

The next phase is bounded by the Uranus opposition during the early forties and/or the Chiron return near age 51. Generally it is the period when our children are adolescents to young adults. We are in a parallel change as we complete parenting and (usually) move into greater freedom. Until now, for most of our lives, many of us have been responsible to or for other people. By the early fifties, we may be alone with ourselves for the first time. If we are married, we may have to restructure the relationship, as responsibilities change.

The period from the Chiron return to the second Saturn Return is (or traditionally has been) a time of facing ourselves. Often truly free to be ourselves for the first time, it can parallel adolescence, in that the rules are changing. Our greatest responsibility is to ourselves.

It is also a time when we begin to contemplate our senior/retirement years. If we are wise, we will begin to consider what we want to do with them, what we want them to mean. Here is where the seeds of a second career are planted. Here is where we begin to think about what we have always wanted to do, whether and how we can manifest that in years to come. Failing that, it is often where health begins to fail.

By the second Saturn return, retirement plans should be formulated. Efforts devoted to career taper off. We have succeeded or not and must accept that and turn our attention to what comes after retirement. By age 75, the next Saturn square, most careers have ended. This is the consultant stage, when our responsibilities to others are only to give advice, and then only upon request. Our primary responsibility is to ourselves.

This is the place where we are designed to complete our own individuation, to be nothing but our true selves and to be all that we can be. We are intended to reach the limits of the current definition of what it means to be human during this period. We are designed to reach full maturity as humans, to be ripe and ready to function beyond the expectations of our birth.

Notice that, at some point during this period, your age exceeds the life expectancy in existence at the time of your birth. If our expectations are limited—if we expect life to be divided between being cared for and caring for others—this period will become just that. It will be a period devoted to the care of the aging—and we will be caring for or being cared for by, (usually) a spouse or our adult offspring.

The final period has no outer limit. It extends from age 84 onward. If we have remained healthy, most people over age 84 are at this point entirely free of restrictions.

We can do even the most outrageous things because we will be indulged based on our age. We now have permission to be as eccentric as we like without undue judgment.

It is also a time when, if we have not done so earlier, we become aware of that which lies beyond the veil. Psychic ability rises, sometimes blocking more rational processes, sometimes being mistaken for senile dementia. Many become forgetful, simply because their attention is on things largely unperceived by the general population.

Still, most of these extraordinary people have attained sufficient wisdom to know whom to trust with their voices and visions. They have become citizens of the cosmos, living beyond the reach of Saturn.

# Contents

# Saturn: The Foundation Under Consciousness

In our research, we could find no discovery date for Saturn, as can be found for the outer planets and Chiron. Many people think that the Bethlehem Star, announcing an avatar for the age of Pisces, was a conjunction of Saturn and Jupiter. While this writer thinks that such a conjunction would need to involve other planets to produce something so spectacular as the New Testament describes, the idea seems valid.

The joint entrance into the general consciousness of the principles represented by Jupiter and Saturn seems quite significant. Jupiter represents expansion, especially the expansion of human consciousness. Above all else, Saturn represents limits. Their joint entry into human consciousness marks the age of Pisces as a limited growth of human consciousness, and/or an expansion of the existing limits on human consciousness.

In any chart, a well-connected Jupiter and Saturn represent a step-by-step process. This one represented the next step in the evolution of humanity. Thus, the avatar, said to have been born under that conjunction, would be the prototype for that measured rise. He would present the idea of a familial relationship with our Creator. He transformed the impersonal Judge Jehovah to our Divine Father. He removed us from the Law of Karma to the Law of Love.

Still, the road was rocky, and progress slow. Jupiter's enthusiasm and love of truth were often curbed and contained by Saturn's limits on our capacity to expand our beliefs. It would take a long time for humanity to discover the difference between a belief and a truth.

The problem—if it is a problem—is inherent in the nature of consciousness, which begins and ends with self-awareness. To become aware of the Self, we must have or create a boundary between Self and Other. Our first act of self-realization must be to shatter the unity, the oneness of all that is. It must be separation from our Source, our Creator, our God/dess. It must be the act of leaving Eden, the Earthly womb from which the Children of God emerged.

The principle of duality began here as here was separated from there, and past from future. With that principle established, logic stepped in to format human consciousness. From that time, all of life was divided into this and/or that. This division is merely a perception, but it is the neces- sary perception for logical thought. Its first task was the naming of things. In giving a thing a name, you give it boundaries. It is this and not that.

The first great mistake of logic was the division of life into good and evil. The second was the association of dark with evil and light with good. In the beginning, the nighttime or dark was not friendly. You could stumble and fall in the dark.

The dark was filled with imperceptible dangers, until humanity learned to make and carry its own light. Predators you could not see might find you in the dark.

In the end, darkness is simply a place in which we cannot see. It is the invisible, the unknown, the place where enlightenment has not yet reached. It should not forbid us entrance, but simply require us to carry a light when we venture there. Until we know that, Saturn will draw a line between light and dark, standing between us and danger. He is our protector, even as he is our jailor.

When considering Saturn, it is important to notice that Jupiter is the planet, and the principle, immediately behind him. Jupiter is the growth principle, and forever pushes Saturn's boundaries outward. As we grow, our skeleton/Saturn and skin/Saturn also grow. Even so, growth in consciousness should expand our limits of belief. Morality should always be predicated on reality. What is not safe for a toddler may be, not merely safe but necessary for an adult. Traditional Saturn's only absolute function is to provide a temporary limit for our protection.

As we should not play with fire until we are mature enough to handle it with respect, even so, certain knowledge should be withheld until a mind is mature enough to respect it. A prime example of this is the body of knowledge, generally called esoteric. This included methods for raising consciousness by energizing the chakras. These were developed as certain individuals began to see energy fields. They observed that more aware individuals had brighter chakras.

They even noticed that certain chakras were associated with certain levels of awareness.

They assumed that a brighter chakra meant a brighter human, so they thought that the way to make humanity more intelligent/aware was to brighten the chakras. And it will work, but can be very hard on the system because it can attract knowledge for which we have no foundation. This is probably what the Master Jesus meant in his parable about a house built upon the sand.

The natural way of energizing chakras is by raising consciousness. The process is one of accumulating information, step by step, building a secure structure for increasingly advanced thinking. As our awareness expands, so are our chakras energized, beginning with the lower ones. As our perceptions widen, our understanding increases, and our vibratory level–translate: the speed of our atoms at the molecular level—increases.[1] Everyone who increases his or her field of awareness, also energizes the chakras that correspond to that area of human consciousness.

A great mistake of the esotericists was making judgments on the chakras. Because the lower chakras are brighter in more primitive people, they assumed that the chakras themselves were more primitive–less evolved.

The chakras are the basis–the foundation–which underlies all expansion of consciousness. The first step in any human process must be survival of the individual (lowest chakra) and the second must be survival of the species, or reproduction (second lowest chakra). Until these areas are secure, consciousness cannot rise much above them.

---

[1] Only those things with an atomic spin at a speed similar to our own will be visible. As our awareness expands, our own atomic motion increases. Some things drop out of our perceptual band and others become visible for the first time.

Only when a species becomes a society can Jupiter raise/expand Saturn's limits into the realms of physics and metaphysics. Only when the mandates of the lower chakras are fulfilled can we attend to higher ones. The age of Pisces has been the bridge–the period during which society evolved from monarchies to democracies, from simple barter to a world economy. Saturn and Jupiter were the authors and progenitors of that period. We are now approaching a new age and a new base level for the general consciousness. The old mission of Saturn and Jupiter has been fulfilled, and now stands as the base for a new development in humanity. Today, the combined efforts of Uranus, Neptune, and Pluto are urging us across the limits of the Solar System, to the galaxy and beyond. Even so Chiron appears on the scene to aid the natural transition of humanity from its adolescence to full adulthood. With the discovery of Eris, we are on our way to becoming more than we can yet imagine.

Physics and metaphysics are coming together as knowledge of the nature and function of the creative consciousness. We are discovering our true spiritual genetics, that we are both physical and spiritual, the heirs of both Earth and Heaven. The ultimate duality is our own makeup. Physicality is not so much a house for spirit, as it is the foundation for the structure which spirit/consciousness will build upon it.

The lesson for the next age, which the esotericists misunderstood, is that human evolution–otherwise known as spiritual growth–is not about freeing spirit from body. In its current phase, it is about Spirit learning to use/Chiron the body, operating through it. It is about making prayer and magic practical. It is about solving their mysteries and making them part of the general knowledge available to all. In doing so, we cross the next great Saturn boundary, becoming more than man. More accurately, we are simply expanding the definition of what it means to be human. We are discovering what has previously lain hidden in the ninety percent of the brain, said to be unused.. Meanwhile, we appear to be activating what has been called junk DNA. Clearly, we have just begun the journey of Self-Discovery. Just as clearly, human potential is much greater than we have believed. All of this is involved in pushing our boundaries, allowing ever-greater self/human awareness.

# The Principle of Limits

# and Boundaries

The traditional definitions of Saturn, still found in older texts, were very much a product of the nearly 18 centuries during which the known planets ended at Saturn's orbit. During that period, Saturn became the symbol of life's dangerous outer limits. If we got too far from home, too close to the edge of the world, we would fall into the abyss.

The symbolism of ancient Saturn took on the coloration of a Satan borrowed from Zoroastrianism and grafted onto Christianity. He became the Discipliner who punished transgressions of the religious law. When Eastern beliefs began to merge with Western ones, Saturn was still a threat–the threat of an unending search for perfection that kept us on the wheel of Karma endlessly.

Where religion gave way to politics, Saturn ruled those aspects of law that punished its transgressors. He was the heavy hand of discipline that would punish us whenever we strayed too far beyond our limits. Laws, rules and the disciplinary measures invested in them become the lines which we might not cross without risking moral, legal, or parental censure. In that sense, Saturn limited and contained our lives.

Saturn boundaries are intended to define how far we may _safely_ go. Our first limits are for physical safety. The newborn is bounded by the space in its crib and playpen. It is also limited by its physical immaturity, which determines goal-oriented movement. We cross a major limit when we learn to crawl, and then to walk. Our limits then expand to the size of a house, a yard, a neighborhood, and so on. Later limits–the ones that trip us up during our adult quests–were set for the comfort of our parents or our society. Their intention was to prevent us escaping or upsetting the status quo, the power of the law, or the control of the church.

A common source of depression in natives with heavy Saturn influences, our tightest, most painful boundaries are those unconscious limits set by family and cultural beliefs and attitudes. These people taught us what it means to be human, to be male or female, to be part of an economic, educational, or cultural group. They set up the parameters for social acceptance. Far too often, staying within those boundaries became the price of love and approval. By word and action, overtly and/or subliminally, the adults in our earliest years set up subtle limits that define our responses and reactions to life, and even our perception of it. From this comes the idea of Saturn as Ego or Conscience. Rules learned as absolutes, before the age of reason (puberty) function as a subliminal control on the spirit. If no one ever broke them, the world would be a stagnant place with the future dying in the present.

These are the ego boundaries that must be overcome, understood, and/or reconditioned if we are to reach our highest goals, dreams, wishes, and potential. When reinforced by painful emotional or physical punishment they may keep us caught in the past, unable to fully individuate. The need to meet the expectations of the past, can divert or destroy the future we intended to have or create. Our very soul is wounded in the process, and we may never notice the scars until some painful transit grabs our attention and focuses it on the wound.

## Bringing Saturn into the Twenty-first Century

Today, with our greater understanding of the nature of human consciousness and its relationship to reality, the essential use of limits emerges. We now know that life is a whole and holographic in nature. However, even knowing that, we cannot entirely grasp it, because our perceptions are not large enough to encompass it. Being, in essence, a part of the whole, we cannot encompass the whole with our minds. When we try to do so, our minds go into overwhelm and blur out.

The first, and most personally significant limits of life, are set by the width of our perceptual bands. How far can we see, and within that distance how much detail do we register? What is the range of sound that we can hear? How sensitive are we to touch, psychic atmosphere and/or emotional tones? How good are our senses of taste, smell and touch? These are the real limits in our world. They define what we call reality. Only as we begin to attain wisdom, do we become truly aware of the fact that the function of senses varies from person to person. More than that, what we perceive as truth or reality varies depending on our perspective. How close are we, and from what angle are we perceiving? Gradually, out of this, we can begin to realize that it is our perceptive function that draws many of the limits that we recognize. Or is it the other way around?

Even more important is the function of limits in the thinking process. We cannot think about large wholes. Instead we must section off an area into which to focus. The act of seeing is really that of not-seeing. It is the ability to focus on a particular area, separating it from the background blur for study. Even so, hearing is more about the ability to sort sound, than it is about the ability to hear it. To a less obvious extent, the same is true of the other senses.

If the human mind is to think at all, it must have the capacity to set some limits, to section off specific subjects, or areas within subjects. Realizing that, we may begin to appreciate the great gifts of Saturn. Even the process of self-realization must begin with sorting ourselves out from our parents, our families, our culture, etc. All sorting is based on division lines, and these are the domain of Saturn.

The expansion of consciousness begins with logic. Logic does not work in an unbounded world. It functions by contrast and comparison. These are derived from defined objects and activities with clear edges and definitions, which are then filed in memory. Even here we have (largely unconscious) rules which set up the file boundaries in our personal data base. Rules are boundaries used to order and contain activity.

Memory files are created and ordered according to rules of function and/or application. Those rules determine the organization of our memory files, in classifications like good-bad, useful-useless, past-present-future, adding application files relative to family-friends- acquaintances-strangers, and so on. How well we can use information we have learned depends on our ability to use the principle of limits in creating an orderly memory-filing system. Memories are most useful when they are sorted into folders and sub-folders for efficient access. Here the Saturn function determines where the lines are drawn between the paragraphs, pages, chapters, documents, and other data-groups in our memory banks. Without Saturn, Chiron's hands are tied, and Neptune can only function through fanciful visions and insubstantial dreams.

**Using Saturn**

Order, whether mental, social, or physical, is based on rules of function, behavior, etc. These are called laws. There are natural laws, moral laws, scientific laws, civil laws. All these are boundary functions. Wherever we draw a line, place a period, finish a project, end a relationship, or graduate from a phase of activity, the limiting Saturn principle is there. Without this principle we would wander through life in a pea-soup fog, so confused that we could not even recognize our own being or name.

The most important thing to be realized about limits is that there are few, if any, <u>absolute</u> <u>limits.</u> A mythical association for Saturn is with Kronos, a Greek god, associated with time. Time is one of the major life limits that we cross. As individuals mature, their personal limits expand. As humanity matures, human limits expand. Maturation occurs primarily through time. In time, the child matures to adulthood. In time, adults acquire wisdom and/or authority.

Through time our outer and inner worlds expand, often exponentially, drawing and redrawing the outlines of reality.

The process of spiritual growth begins with individuation, and then comes full circle, returning to unity. Again, time is involved, and progress is often bounded by the length of a lifetime. Still, as we widen and deepen our ranges of perception and thought, we cross even that boundary and begin to view life as that which exists beyond time and space, unlimited and free. But, lest we get lost in eternity and/or an endless cosmos, we learn to view it in part, even while remaining aware of the whole. This is the great lesson Saturn has to teach us.

Always and forever, the only thing that limits any of us, is the range of our consciousness, and that range is only limited by our personal evolutionary state. As we mature, awareness expands. We may sense more, feel more, know more, be more. One by one, we cross every limit we have ever known.

*As students of Astrology and Life, one of the most beneficial things you can do for your life is to rename Saturn as a temporary limit set for a specific, knowable purpose.* Another is to question every idea you take as law. Change your definition of law to a scientific one. Make it merely a description of the way something works. Keep in mind that science continually discovers new and more expanded versions of the natural laws. Question and analyze your laws and boundaries. Make them flexible and changeable. Use this principle as a tool, not an end.

The modern astrologer is probably not an astronomer, as were the ancients. Today, most serious professional astrologers have some knowledge of psychology and metaphysics. As eternally occurs, the Jupiter principle of expansion has pushed Saturn's limits outward. Still, the containment symbolized by Saturn, prevents undisciplined growth, giving us time to assimilate change. Their partnership is a great gift to humanity, permitting it to move ever upward and onward, one step at a time. It is time to recognize and honor Saturn as a guardian angel, keeping watch over the maturation process of humanity.

# Metaphysical Saturn

# Consciousness and Spirituality

Technically, a boundary is a concentration of particles/energy which is used to contain energy, converting it into form. Limits curb, direct, define, or stop the flow of energy as action. . If, instead of seeing a roadblock in life, we see a temporary resting place, an outline, container or channel for energy, we will have renamed the Saturn function in a positive way.

The problem that we sometimes have is that Original Being or spirit has no very solid idea of boundaries or limits because it is an essentially unbounded and unlimited energy. Still, if energy is to take form, it must have boundaries, and if it is to have purpose, it must have limits.

In the realms of pure metaphysics, we run into difficulties because at that level EVERYTHING is energy/spirit. We try to contain spirit within spirit. It is this difficulty that underlies the general belief that a body is a container for a spirit . . . and viewed from ordinary levels of consciousness it is.

Ultimate Being does have certain "structural boundaries" and even limits of expression. Without them there can be no sense of self, as differentiated from not-self, and it is this sense of self that is most clearly our spiritual heritage. The realization of self, of identity, is a boundary. Even to say "I am an unbounded being" suggests some (probably unconscious) boundaries because without an ending place or an "I am not," there can be no true recognition of I AM. In the spiritual being, the difference is that boundaries are taken for granted as a quality of being and given no further attention--so they are not, or at least do not feel, limiting.

We do not know where the structural limits of Ultimate Being are because we have no capacity to expand our personal consciousness to that extent; we become overwhelmed because focusing on those limits requires us to shift awareness too far from our own limits. We then lose our sense of a personal self as distinct from other Terran life forms. To completely lose self would be to lose form. We would disappear . . . or float off earth . . . or get "beamed up" into some other reality where we would (at least seem to) be someone different with a different sense of self or identity derived from the context of a different reality.

Wherever life differentiates between self and not-self, there are boundaries. These boundaries make human consciousness possible. Consciousness is a process of continually refining the self-image through separating the self from the not-self, to more firmly establish a self-concept solid enough to present a self-image. This, in turn, must be solid enough to function as an identity. Modern computers, with their abilities to handle data bases, are magnificent images of the process of self-realization. Theoretically, you could have all the inhabitants of earth in a data bank that could be sorted in various ways, continually reducing the data base from which selections were being made until you finally reduced it to a single individual: yourself.

This is a process of adding limits. When you have all the limits in place, you have a definition of yourself. Your name becomes a shorthand term for that definition. Having a clear definition or sense of self, you will also have a vast, secondary data base which includes information about what is required to keep you in your right body and mind. You will know what you need, what you seek to become, do, have, learn, teach, express. It will tell you what kind of energy you radiate, what your function in life is and how you work at it. Perhaps most important of all, it shows how you relate to all other persons, places, things, ideas, ideals, dreams and structures, visible or invisible.

Contrary to the "old" astrological notions of a negative, satanic, Saturn, he serves a very important, even a required function in life. The more we love our limits, the better they will serve us. Like anything else which is living, limits respond to praise by growing, changing, expanding. Correspondingly, to criticism by contracting, losing energy, and dying. Continual criticism will squeeze the spirit out of a thing, converting all its energy to rock solid form and immovability. It may then die, disintegrate, and have its elements reused in another process; or it may continue to exist for a time, but will not truly live. It will no longer truly be human and able to recognize its essential nature and spirit.

Here, we see the flip side of the combined entry of Jupiter/expansion with Saturn/limits into the general consciousness. The Jupiterian ability to understand the principles of consciousness allows recognition of the value of limits. Like the ability to expand, the recognition of limits is entirely a matter of belief. As spiritual, and therefore essentially unlimited, beings, the only limits we can have are those which we regard as necessary, valuable, or useful for identity, creativity and enlightenment.

## Saturn: Container for Life

The only place where limits truly exist is in consciousness. We hold group definitions of life in the general or world consciousness. We have generally accepted limits of human abilities based on

---

[2]Most purpose involves the expansion of limits; with no limits to expand, it is impossible to conceive of a purpose . . . or even any real livingness.

[3]The similarity of nmes is not coincidence.

Metaphyiscal Saturn

our definition of human beingness. Historically, most of these were regarded as physical and/or what makes the physical acceptable to its spiritual source, so that it can be allowed to return home.

One of the most valuable life-tools that can be learned from the study of astrology is the nature and purpose of limits. The principle has several aspects. Two are of primary importance.

The first of these is that life processes are self-limiting. This can easily be observed in human growth processes. We, quite naturally, stop growing physically when our bodies reach a size that is adequate for our purpose. We do not have to do anything to stop it. There is also a limiting of the reproductive phase in females so that conception does not generally occur before or after the period when women are most physically able to carry a fetus to term. Other limits are defined in terms of internal maturation. Most children learn to communicate near the same age, and they begin to reason during another fairly specific period.

Limits are inherent in being. What a thing is–meaning how we define it, will determine its boundaries and limits. These  will remain relatively constant unless we do major work in consciousness to change them. The only real way to expand our limits beyond the accepted norm is to rename and redefine ourselves. Only an expanded consciousness can do so.

We, individually, and as a species, are given certain boundaries and limits in the same way that parents set limits for growing children—according to the development of the child.  Even so humanity and life. Each phase of life, each species, has certain limits of development and/or purpose. When those limits have been reached, the species dies or it mutates, adapting to a new purpose or environmental developments.

When consciousness expands sufficiently(Jupiter function), we achieve the capacity to begin setting our own limits and boundaries. Having reached adulthood, we no longer ask or expect our parents to choose our boundaries. Spiritual maturation also brings greater responsibility and new boundaries. While individuals can move out ahead of the general consciousness, there is a limit to how far ahead they may go—at any one time. There is one very graphic example in today's society.

When Jesus walked the earth, one of the most significant statements he made was this: The things that I do, ye shall do, and greater things.[4] One  thing he did was to raise the dead, by the power of his word.  Today the dead are raised daily, through mechanical means! We have trusted the command but not the method.  We set limits on our abilities, allowing only a few individuals to do it, and then only with the proper training and apparatus.

The possibility of healing, and even reviving dead bodies, entered human consciousness some two thousand years ago. Still, we have set limits on our willingness to take the awesome responsibility for changing or extending the lives of others. With the god-abilities go the god- responsibilities and, in general, we do not yet feel ready to assume them.  Let there be no condemnation in that, it is our choice--an opportunity not a command.

Learning continues in phases. We have passed through many of these phases even in the face of learned religious beliefs which threaten us with eternal condemnation.  Rather than condemning the authors and perpetrators of these beliefs, let us bless them for the service they have done in helping us through our "childhood." Surely, they are no more to be condemned than the parents of adult children who cling to the parental role because they have no other concept of themselves, having set personal limits by defining themselves only in terms of parenting.

Much religious doctrine has become obsolete, even as the function of parents becomes obsolete when the children reach adulthood. Still it behooves us to give credit where credit is due, and to be as kind as we can. The past is the foundation on which the future is built. However, if the species is to survive, we cannot allow the past to set limits on the future. When it attempts to do so, we are required to set personal limits that exclude it.

## Saturn Today

Today, many of us have evolved to a place of conscious identification with the spirit of love. Like Original Being, we see no evil and cannot imagine that anyone would want to limit life, or hate it. Still, there are those who do. There are those who have set their own boundaries rigidly, from fear or pride. These resist and control the flow of life. It retaliates by becoming a destructive force—like anti-matter, perhaps. It is in this sense—and this sense only—that Saturn/limits might be called a Satanic or evil force. When Saturn overrules Jupiter, he becomes an antithesis to life, bringing death by suffocation. He literally smothers life and consciousness.

Even here, the fixation of limits may prove to be the mediating force, for, very often, the limits themselves have limits, and such beings are allowed to begin again in some other time- space continuum. If they are truly interfering in ways that harm others, it may fall to us to speak a prayer or affirmation which will remove them from our space, blessing them on their way to their own highest good.

Astrologically, Uranus comes to the aid of those whose personal and spiritual growth is hindered by Saturn. Wherever boundaries get too rigid, too limiting, the next transit of Uranus will break their hold by removing whatever person or circumstance we have used to keep us bound.

Responsibility is generally regarded as a heavy Saturnian limit. Although used to limit us with duty, it is intended to mean responsiveness. We are morally responsible to and for our children and our own lives. We usually take responsibility for our property. Outside these parameters, most responsibility is dealt out by people who intend to control us with guilt. No adult is ever responsible for the health, happiness, or needs of another adult! If they claim that you are, run!

In the area of employment, responsibility is highly prized. Here it means that we and our word can be relied upon, that we will take appropriate leadership and finish what we start. This type of responsibility is a component of success—another Saturn word.

Rights come with such responsibilities. We have the right to have our boundaries respected (another Saturn term). In this country, we say that my rights end where yours begin and that we are free to do anything that does not interfere with the rights of another. This is expressed in Wicca as:

An ye harm none, do as you will. In Christianity it is: Do unto others as ye would that men should do unto you. It is called the Golden Rule and appears, in some form, in every moral or ethical system known to this author. It may then be considered a spiritual principle, a simple declaration of spiritual rights, and a guiding principle of life.

Interpersonal boundaries are not so much a matter of morality or ethics, as one of practicality. Where I set the limits of acceptable behavior for myself is where I may expect others to limit theirs. This is an incredibly practical approach that, if generally practiced, would eliminate the need for most government.

It has, however, been widely misinterpreted. Its shadow, or reverse side has been largely ignored by the religious community. Far too many of us have been taught that while it is not all right to trespass on another, it is all right to allow them to trespass on us. In its most virulent form, this belief invites rape, burglary, and murder, thus creating "saints" who are, more accurately, victims. Such a path draws far too many truly good people into a pattern that is destructive to life. The antidote to this "sickness unto death" is simply this:

1. If we are spiritual beings, if we are the offspring of Original Being, then allowing ourselves to be violated, also allows our god/dess to be violated. We have no right to permit such abuse. Still many are conditioned to believe that they have no right, and often no ability, to fight back. The solution is always to set some personal boundaries.

2. If we have moved our identification from "merely human" to the realization

that we are "god/dess beings" we may then realize that where such a one dwells is heaven—or a temple—or within a magic circle, and that such acts are not permitted in such spaces.

3. If we allow these others to continue in such behavior, we are supporting their dependency, creating co-dependant relationships that do not contribute to the growth of either party because both are reduced to a survival mode. Neither will advance. If we support the resistance of others to growth—literally to living—we also support their progression toward death. This is hardly responsible behavior and clearly neither loving nor logical.

4. Since we are loving beings, we must follow the example of many birds and "kick them out of the nest" so that they can/will learn to fly. Doing this, we have no assurance that they will, but we do have the assurance that we have done our best for them—no matter what they or anyone else may say. Sometimes love means abandonment and that kind of love takes a great deal of courage, but we do have that if we will but call on it.

# The Modern Saturn Dynamic

# and Applications

**Saturn as Ruler of Capricorn and the Tenth House**

As Saturn is a symbol for individual maturity, so Capricorn is a symbol for human maturity. Capricorn represents the outer limits of the <u>current</u> definition of the species called Human. That definition includes human abilities and possibilities. Any Capricorn planet or point in a personal horoscope enters incarnation already bumping against that definition.

Consequently, such areas can feel like no growth is possible and the result can be depression. Only when we realize two things, can we push past the current limits. First, we must recognize all limits as temporary and intended to move outward. Second, we must realize that the definition of what it means to be human is included in that statement. We are all destined to become more than man (as currently defined). How much more can be projected from the scientific estimate that most people use only about 10 per cent of their brain.

As ruler of the tenth house, Saturn defines the limits of expectation, as seen from our birth. While it may later represent our social goals, it initially represents the expectations of the adults in our childhood–expectations that we often struggle to fulfill. It becomes our public image–what we look like to the general public.

The Midheaven is the noon-point or apex of our chart–not the end, but the high point, relative to society. It has a strong connection with the second Saturn Return and retirement from the social phase. When we make an avocation or career of what we love, that falls in the eleventh house. We are just beginning to realize that some of us can, and may be intended to, skip over the tenth house, going directly to the eleventh, where our spiritual goals lie.

**Orbital Boundaries**

The journey of any planet, from one transit of the sign it rules to the next, represents a cycle of development. Technically, we refer to a full orbit around the Sun, as perceived from Earth, and it is a personal choice to view them as beginning and ending with their own sign. These cycles vary in length from about one month for the Moon, one year for the Sun, Mercury, and Venus, two years for Mars, and 12 for Jupiter up to two hundred fifty two years for Pluto.

Saturn makes the circle from any point to its next crossing of the same point in about twenty-nine and a half years. When it recrosses its natal position in your chart, we call it a Saturn Return.

Saturn recrossing Capricorn, is a symbolic return for Humanity, signifying the point where the circular orbit rises into a metaphysical spiral. Every Saturn passage through Capricorn marks a new median level of maturity in humanity. Most especially, it signifies a new baseline in individuals being born.

Saturn last entered Capricorn near the beginning of 1989. Children born since then have the creative side of consciousness fully activated. Whatever you make them believe, they will demonstrate. Beware teaching these children that their expanded consciousness means that they are crazy or evil, lest they show you what that means! Fortunately, today, fewer adults are making children wrong for having wider perceptual bands than their parents and grandparents had.

Some obvious effects of the new awareness can be seen by observing television programming. First aliens and space travel debuted, followed in short order by holograms, angels, witches, and psychics. Clearly those subjects are rising to the surface of human consciousness, bringing their own questions and answers.

## Saturn Transits

The simplest way of understanding Saturn transits is to regard them as opportunities to rename or redefine the planet or point being transited. When Saturn transits a natal planet, the nodal axis, the horizon or meridian of the chart, you are being asked to refine the point being transited. Its journey across each house is an opportunity to redefine the workings of that house, to give it a meaning that is more relevant to your current maturity level.

When Saturn transits are painful, it is because they are pointing out boundaries that are limiting us. It is time to expand those boundaries, to learn, or be, or do something new–something that takes us beyond our old boundaries. This may feel risky. We are moving into new territory, new experience.

In one way or another, these transits are also about breaking habits, although they may be emotional, perceptual, or habits of belief, rather than physical habits. For example: If we have a habit of losing our temper, a Saturn transit to Mars urges us to look beneath our angry responses, to find the fear that underlies them. The next step may be one of realizing that we are now adults and have nothing to fear from the persons or situations that have been triggering our anger. This will free Mars energy for more creative pursuits.

Generally, Saturn *conjunctions* indicate a thorough redefinition of the point being crossed. An *opposition* from Saturn confronts us with outside limits. They represent periods when other individuals or society-in-general seems to limit us. Examples: People who guilt-trip us, a slow economy. *Squares* and *semi-squares* cause us to trip over some limit—often a limit of belief like "I don't have enough education," or "I don't have enough money."

*Sextiles* and *trines* from Saturn move us beyond old boundaries smoothly and easily. We may get excited by, or engrossed in, some activity and only realize that we have crossed a boundary after the fact. *Quintiles* and *deciles* expand Saturn limits by revealing some previously unrecognized ability or talent. Example: When the author spontaneously began to channel additional information into her horoscope readings, transiting Saturn was sextile her natal Moon and quintile her natal Neptune. (Several other transiting aspects added support, as is usual with quintiles.)

## Saturn Qualifiers

*Retrograde Saturn* individuals have greater maturity than others with their sign placement. They are more self-responsible, less dependant even as children, than direct Saturns. They are also more responsive to feelings and might be called empaths. Between their own loneliness and their desire to alleviate the pain they feel from others, they are easy targets for human parasites. At some point, they must learn tough love and how to say, "No, thou shalt not!"

The boundaries represented by *intercepted Saturn* are unconscious, often because they are so far out as to be more galactic than Earthly and they blur, even become transparent. We do not learn them from our father, or any other human authority. Instead, we seem to inherit them from our mother in the bonding process. As hers extend beyond the horizon, so do ours. More accurately, the mother-child connection is based on the Venus principle, "Like attracts like." In the mean time, the lack of male influence produces over-bonding and your life lesson will be about learning to distinguish your own needs from the needs of others in bonded relationships.[5]

Intercepted Saturn looks like a lack of fathering or a lack of discipline. More literally, it refers to a childhood environment in which limits were taken for granted to such an extent that no one told this child where they were. We were required to define personal limits through observation of other family members. Without well-defined personal boundaries, we are very aware. We notice that parents have different limits from each other, from their children, from other adults, and/or they may set different limits for different siblings.

## Saturn Returns: Graduation Time

Saturn is the polar partner of the Moon. The Moon flows, cycles, and generally handles the energy flow through life. An easy, unconscious flow needs boundaries for direction, and Saturn provides them. He is the banks of the stream.

As we become increasingly conscious, the energy flow increases and our boundaries must stretch or give way. When they do not[6], life is cramped or dammed up with resulting pain or lack.

[5]Your mother, your children, and your sexual partners.
[6]Showed by negative aspects to the Moon from Saturn limits or Pluto controls.

Cycles provide timing devices for predictive work. For cycles to have meaning, we must recognize them as having beginnings and endings. Saturn symbolizes our definition of these cycles and marks the significant points in them. Together they present us with a means of dividing our lives into manageable segments. Without this capacity we might be overwhelmed.

Saturn's own cycles—transits relative to his natal place—provide the outlines of our lives. They measure our developing maturity.

## The First Saturn Return

Most people experience the crossing between the first and second maturation cycles during the year before their thirtieth birthday. Common events of this period are marriage, divorce, or the birth of a child. These clearly and obviously show a change of responsibility, but their meaning is symbolic.

During the first 30 years of our lives, our parents' responsibility for our lives gradually decreases. Around age 21, we may be officially emancipated, but as we move into our own careers and establish our own families, we are usually still following our parents' rules, living within their definitions of what or how we should be. Some marry or have children from the subconscious intention to confine themselves to the duties assigned to them by their families, religion, and/or culture. This transition is often painful because we are in a major internal, and sometimes external, power struggle with the authorities of our childhood. Early marriages may fall apart at this time, because we married for reasons not our own. Having done so, we may feel restricted by our mate or our marriage.

Entering the new cycle, we usually exchange our family rules for society's rules. We struggle to fulfill society's expectations. We try to do what everyone else is doing. Often this phase becomes an endurance contest. Many endure in an inappropriate relationships and/or hang onto jobs they hate because the society we live in expects it. Saturn's greatest hazard is inertia. We resist change, afraid to break the rules, or become our own authority

Spiritually, the first Saturn return grants us the right to set our own rules, within the context of society. Our only real limits are the contracts that we make. *The only non-revocable contract we can make is to our children.* When we choose to have children---whether consciously or unconsciously we are assuming a spiritual obligation to them. However, like any contract, this one has an end. Our financial obligation, and our right to set limits for them, ends with the emancipation of our children. Our obligation or right to advise them ends as they approach age thirty. Then, we must grant them equality in rank, ending our advisory role in their lives. After that we are merely an information resource to be used only by their own choice.

## The Second Saturn Return

The second Saturn return usually occurs near the fifty-ninth birthday. Its significance is graduation from social demands. By this time most of us have completed responsibilities to our children

The Modern Saturn Dynamic and Applications

and we have reached the pinnacle of our career. Whether or not we have met our own criterion for success, at this time we stop struggling to climb its ladder.

This is the astrological retirement age, and some do manage to retire at that age. Those, who do not actually do so, cease the struggle for the top, realizing that it is time to turn down the hill, and let the next generation pass by. Some experience relief and feel free to go play or begin a second career, doing something that they have long wished to do. Others experience profound disappointment or depression at the thought of losing their conditioned role in society. Many of the latter resign from earth within a few years. Those who do not may regress into senility.

Metaphysically, the second Saturn Return grants us the right to make our own rules within the context of humanity. At this point, we step beyond the boundaries of society, and are generally free of our contractual obligations. Even if some of our contracts are not entirely fulfilled, we are free to make no new contracts. No longer are we required to think about the physical survival of humanity. Instead we turn our faces to issues of spirit and/or individuality. We assume the right and the responsibility to make our own moral and ethical choices. Here we truly experience our own authority, deferring to no other human. At this time the status of Wise One, Crone, and/or Honored Grandparent, granted near age fifty-one and our Chiron return, becomes real. In modern terms, we become a consultant.

## The Third Saturn Return

The third Saturn return usually occurs during the year before age 89. At this time we graduate from a world view to a galactic or evolutionary view. We resign our position as consultant, freeing our consciousness from the boundary between this world and the next.

It is common for elderly people to begin napping frequently at this time, but many are simply slipping out of body to explore what lies beyond this world of experience. Some, who are unable to endure the strangeness of this, remain present, but slip into a second childhood. There are other ways of deferring the choice to leave earth. While the astral traveler is looking forward to a higher realm, the senile dementia victim is regressing to an earlier state. Those in the latter group lack the courage, <u>or</u> are unaware of their ability, to rise.

Meanwhile, the mentally flexible, allow their vision to expand to even greater awareness. While physical senses often deteriorate, the interior senses continue to expand. Losing sight, hearing, or mobility is simply a method of turning these functions inward. It is based on an assumption of bandwidth limits. Instead of realizing that perceptual bands can and do expand, most of these elders simply change their focus. They stop seeing, or hearing, the physical realm while they explore the previously invisible one.

During this period, most develop or increase inner abilities--clairaudience, clairvoyance, and/or clairsentience. Some natives direct these abilities into high-quality writing or art, becoming channels of inspiration to the world.

Metaphysically, the third Saturn Return is a graduation from a world view to a galactic view. Their focus-point moves off-world to a place where they can mediate between the divine state and the human state. These are the real prophets of this world and role models for earlier Saturn generations. They are pushing the limits of usefulness as set by the general consciousness.

## The Fourth Saturn Return

While this writer knows of no one who has achieved this graduation, she has several clients/ friends who are working toward it. Life expectancy is rising rapidly, so someone we know is certain to pioneer this level of achievement soon.

The fourth Saturn Return is predicted for the year before age 118. At this time, consciousness expands again and we graduate to a cosmic view. One reason the achievement of this age has been delayed is that our belief systems have not included the possibility of achieving such a state while in a physical body. Only recently have those people leading the advance into the Aquarian Age become accustomed to the idea of channeling information from one time/space to another. The idea of living from a viewpoint beyond time and space is almost impossible to grasp. It is probably not going to happen with any frequency until we move entirely into the next age, because it is a prophecy of the state to be achieved in the age beyond that. While from our perspective, it is a Neptunian State, the age to which we will next be looking toward (after Aquarius) is Capricorn. Combining those, we see that the role will be that of a Master Being and its function will be managership of the human course of destiny. Most of us are not ready for that yet.

Still, we who are presently crossing the end of the second Saturn cycle into the third, have made such a major transformation in our notions of human limits that we can sense possibilities that extend far into the future. Given the opportunity to talk with a few people who are crossing into the fourth cycle, we can push our thinking out to fuzzy horizons of future possibilities where fifth and sixth Saturn Returns may be experienced.

# Saturn and Your Birth Chart,

# Generally

**Legal Limits**

At the social level, Saturn is The Law. Here the evolutionary process has moved from tribal law to monarchies to democracy. Today our official rights end where those of the next person begin. We have defined property rights and laws to manage our behavior in public areas and especially in traffic-ways. Here the Saturn-principle protects everyone, their rights and their property. In essence, the governmental structures of the world are all Saturnian, but some have a Jupiterian balance which guards personal freedoms and some are out of balance, with certain elements running rampant over the basic rights of others.

**Limits of Function**

At the scientific level, Saturn is a different kind of law, based on observation. There are laws of physics, many of which are now being transcended by laws of metaphysics. Out of particle physics has come quantum theory which explains the creative side of consciousness. Where we once said, "I will believe it when I see it," we are now learning that belief affects reality. Today, we are recognizing belief as a major limit on our lives. You will never see what you do not look for, what you do not believe exists.

Consciousness–the ability to be aware–continually rises in the Human Species. Awareness builds on awareness as external data banks and inner senses expand. The Law of Evolution rules whether it is accepted or not. Today, the evolution in human consciousness is difficult to overlook.

In 1988 transiting Saturn entered Capricorn. The two and a half years that followed brought the traditional definition of what it means to be human to a close. By the time Saturn entered Aquarius at the beginning of 1991, many people had begun to accept intuitive and psychic abilities as normal. Television played a significant role by adding aliens, angels, and various psychic phenomena to their programming. By the beginning of the third millennium, even professional psychics began to be televised.

At first, the effect of this redefinition on the children born at that time went unnoticed. Gradually, intuitives, then adult caretakers, began to notice that most children born were different from earlier generations.

## Psychological Limits

During the past century, a great deal was learned about human psychology. We began to understand the roles of parents in the development of individuals as never before. Certain interpersonal dynamics looked like laws. Then came the arrival of Indigo and Crystal children, who seem to break many of our psychological laws. Out of this comes a true sense of Saturn's purpose. His boundaries are always temporary. They are intended only to keep us from venturing too far, too fast. Never, were they meant to be rigid or unchanging.

Psychological limits are composed largely of the no-nos given to children. Adults tell children that they cannot do certain things because they are not big enough, smart enough, pretty enough, etc. Sometimes they say that we talk too much, want too much, need too much, ask too many questions, make too much noise, or too many messes. Artistic talents may go undeveloped because we are taught that it does not pay, that we must be practical. Natural intuitives are treated as learning disabled because they have answers for which they cannot explain the source or the method by which they arrived at this conclusion. The list goes on.

All too often these limits actually belong to the parents, who assume that their children will inherit their limits. In recent decades the generation gap is wider than it has ever been, largely because of the invention of radio, then television, then calculators, followed by personal computers. The most recent expansion has been the linking of telephone, satellite, and computer technology which now allows individuals access to world-wide data bases.

## Religious and Ethical Limits

Even so the moral laws of religion and philosophy. While some inalienable rights exist, most moral laws should also be regarded as temporary boundaries. Humans do evolve and mature, and so does the world. There was a time when the world was sparsely settled. Religious law mandated fertile marriages. The law made sense at the time, although for reasons largely unknown or unconscious. Only when the world reached a certain population, could it reach a level of civilization which permitted the general population time to think. It is, always and forever, people who have time to think, to wonder, to question, who expand the general level of consciousness in humanity.

Today, certain moral laws drive people into lifestyles that harness their greatest gifts to the service of a religious imperative that makes no sense in an increasingly over-populated world. Worse, the general population has accepted as fact the need for one-to-one commitments. The result is marriages that are killing the spirit of the people in them, a high divorce rate, and children growing up in a world which no longer properly values them.

Here we see a dramatic example of a stubborn Saturn, refusing Jupiterian growth. By the laws of life, Uranus must intervene, before we have turned our world into starving wilderness. If readers think that more catastrophic events are happening now, it may simply be Uranian forces, breaking up obsolete Saturn boundaries lest they strangle us.

**Saturn-Jupiter Aspects**

Wherever the expansive (Jupiter) energy manifests, look for some boundary or limit—preferably a temporary and moveable one. When the two work together they produce a kind of controlled growth process, similar to the idea of moving through phases or climbing steps. The advantage of steps over smooth inclines is that there is far less likelihood of regression when one is allowed to pause for breath or for review, or to consolidate gains regularly.

**Saturn and the Moon**

Our natal Moon directs the flow of Solar (spirit) energy through our lives. Compare this energy flow to the physical circulatory system. A body, through which no energy flows is dead. Fluid energy is symbolized by Water, perhaps because it has many of the same qualities. Water needs limits, to prevent it from meandering without purpose. It does not run up hill very well, being subject to a rollover or wave effect. Only when converted to ice will it stay in place; only when converted to steam will it naturally rise.

Any element with a natural tendency to flow requires boundaries, if it is to function as a form, a structure, an idea, a concept, a being, or a unit. Image Saturn as the safety net for growth, the container in which creation takes place, the ground in our electrical system, the banks of our stream of consciousness. The interplay between the natal Moon and natal Saturn has a lot to do with physical health and/or a healthy lifestyle. Negative aspects between the two show boundaries that must be dealt with as a part of our maturation process. They may be expanded, re-defined, removed, or gone around, but they cannot be ignored. The process always begins with understanding that such boundaries once served a purpose. In some way they protected us.

# Saturn and Your Birth Chart,

# Specifically

At the beginning of life, Saturn is our *Authority Figure.* From this comes the tradition of Saturn as Father, because Father was the nominal head-of-the family, its business manager, chairman of discipline, the family provider and protector. Even when Mother handled day to day discipline problems, Father was regarded as the final authority, if only because of his larger size and deeper voice.

For the past several generations, family structures have been changing. Many fathers are missing, psychologically or physically, but children still need authority figures, because they need to know that someone is responsible for their safety and security.

The Authority Figure is usually the person officially responsible for the financial support of the family–probably the person with the largest income–certainly the person in charge of providing for the family.[7] If not the maker of rules, the Authority Figure is the final court of appeals in disciplinary matters. An Authority Figure may be someone whom you look up to and admire.

Alternatively, the official authority figure may hang over your head. Such a one is an abuser, not an administrator of discipline. *Discipline cannot be learned from an undisciplined parental figure.*

The sign, house and condition of Saturn describe your authority figure. Only when Saturn and the Sun are in compatible signs and/or positive aspect is Father the authority figure. With Saturn in Cancer or conjunct the Moon, it is Mother. Pluto-Scorpio may be a grandparent, Jupiter- Sagittarius may be The Church, Capricorn is older, to suggest a few. Leo may be someone acting as an Authority (having usurped authority?), while Virgo is one functioning as an Authority— someone to whom authority is delegated, as a babysitter. Always look to the context of the chart.

---

[7]Dad may send child-support, but if he stops, the responsibility falls on Mom. (Yes, this can reverse, but that is still relatively rare.)

## Personal Space Boundaries

*Saturn also describes our Personal Space Boundaries* which many believe to represent larger invisible bodies that exist as adjuncts to the physical one. Probably these have something to do with fields of energy radiation. They have a certain sensitivity, like added senses that have their own levels of development and may be "higher" or "lower" than those of the physical body.

Having these boundaries touched or crossed has effects that we feel, and if the crossing is not by our choice, it will feel like a violation. Saturn rules these, so is often involved in descriptions of abuse, as a violation of (personal space) boundaries.

A Saturn very close to the Sun or Ascendant may indicate an adult who invades your space during childhood. This may result in your building "psychic walls" that may have to come down later in life.

Saturn in Pisces and/or conjunct Neptune indicates weak boundaries—most of which are accompanied by the violations of abuse. This usually indicates a lack of protection. We may then spend a significant period in a victim mode. Alternatively, we learn that our faith can protect us.

## Psychological Limits

By sign, Saturn represents our Psychological Limits. House placements and aspects may modify these, to show where they are most active, and often why we are limited in this way. Some more obvious limits are Saturn in Taurus/Money, in Virgo/Guilt, in Sagittarius—by your beliefs. These need conversion Taurus Saturn is authorized to make money. Virgo Saturn is actually innocent and needs only practice in managing its own life. Sagittarian beliefs must be realized as just that—beliefs, not truth. They may then be expanded as wisdom.

Initially, these limits were intended to protect us, in the same way that crib railings and yard fences do. Saturn was there to keep us from getting run over, drowned, overwhelmed, over stimulated, etc. In essence, he represented the container for our life. Because of that, Saturn is linked to both the skeletal structure and the skin. However, these continually grow. As they do, so should our personal boundaries also grow.

The difficulty is that, along with boundaries which actually served to protect our immature selves from harm, we also acquired certain boundaries designed to protect us from emotional injury. Much depended on the level of spiritual maturity in our caretakers. Some adult subtly threaten their children with abandonment for any displays of independence and/or maturity. In a modern world, boundaries often serve to keep us confined within the expectations of our early authority figures. One of the great difficulties today, is that many of us have no well-defined boundary between our childhood and our adulthood. All too often, as adults, we periodically trip over boundaries that should have been moved, even eliminated, years before.

# Saturn in the Houses

It is important to realize that the house placement of Saturn (or any planet) refers to environmental conditioning. In Saturn's house the voice of our Authority Figure is loud. It is the parental voice that may haunt our adulthood for years. The threat of disapproval and/or punishment is attached to it.

Saturn does not set an inherent limit on a house, but it does set a conditioned one. Reaching adulthood, in one way or another, we must take back our authority in that house. We must claim the right to make and live by our own rules.

The necessity to reclaim our authority, to claim our adulthood and its rights, is strongest in the generations born before 1970-80. We refer to the generations which preceded the New Kids—meaning nearly everyone born before 1970, many before 1980, and a few born later than that.

---

Indigos and Crystals have a natural sense of authority and do not submit easily to having parents assert traditional parental rights. Authoritarian adults trigger aggressive responses in Indigos, while Crystals will simply ignore parental dictates, as though they went unheard. No parent of an Indigo will get away with explanations like "because I said so," or "because I am bigger." Neither will they get away with lies, deception or manipulation.

Wise parents will respect their children's right to be who they are. While some limits are necessary for young children, these must be reasonable and they must be explained. Rules must be set for the safety of the children and the sanity of parents.

Parents must earn, give and expect respect. This includes explaining the reasons for the rules they make, the limits they set. Even if the explanation is that the parents need children to comply for the comfort of the parents, children will respect the honesty.

When parents try to live by traditional, authoritarian parenting ideas, the house delineations given will become family battlefields and/or areas of frustration for natives and their parents.

SPECIAL NOTE: "New Kids" commonly have Saturn in one of the first six houses, especially the first three, because their personal authority is strong.

---

### Saturn Conjunction the Ascendant

Your self-image belongs to your authority figure and you may look like him or her. You identify with this person and may have no self-image of your own. This limits your ability to express your true self (your Sun). If Saturn is in the twelfth house, this will be unconscious, taken for granted, and you will not question it for a long time. If in the first house, it will be much more obvious. As you mature you must decide whether to be limited by it. It will be important to remember that "looking like another" and "being like another" are not the same thing. Inherited abilities can be used in new ways.

### Saturn in the First House

This shows limits on the self-image. This comes from being expected to stay within bounds set by adults. These bounds are usually created and enforced by handing us responsibilities that ordinarily belong to adults.

We look mature and are called old for our age. Usually we are called a responsible child, and/or a small adult. Sometimes this means only that we take the responsibility for setting our own rules. We are then self-disciplined—or not[8]—from an early age. This can happen for a variety of reasons, but suggests adults who lack either the time or the inclination to discipline their children.

Most commonly, this refers to an older child who is an assistant parent, assistant housekeeper or maintenance person. We are expected to be responsible for other people and/or for tasks normally performed by adults. This responsibility confines us to being that, limiting our self- awareness by keeping our focus narrow. When you do not have time to think, your spiritual growth suffers.

### Saturn in the Second House

This sets limits on self-worth.  You are conditioned to depend on your own resources and to regard them as limited. Here the abilities of a child are judged by adult standards.

Natives are usually expected to earn the right to the good things in life. Often made some type of servant or family employee, their self-worth is limited to what they can earn in terms of attention, appreciation and/or money.

In one sense or another, they are self-supporting from an early age. Like first house Saturns, they take on adult responsibilities. Unlike them, rewards are available for doing so.

Where first house Saturns are ordered to take responsibility, second house Saturns are coerced into it. They are rewarded with attention, approval and/or money. This can fix your boundaries, as though set in cement because imposed limits are accepted as values.

This placement also suggests that the Authority Figure is a personal asset who controls the purse strings and the approval. This can set you up for financial limits during your adult years if  the decision about whether you have earned the right to affluence remains in the hands of authority figures.

---

[8]Consider the sign placement.

## Saturn in the Third House

This limits communication and/or education. This is a "shut up, you don't know what you're are talking about" placement. It implies assigned limits on what you may think, speak or question. The authority figure demands unquestioned adherence to his or her beliefs. It is the "because I said so . . . " placement.

Usually this drives all the questions inward, with an end result of intuitive development. However the emotional side of these limits may set natives up to be poor elementary, and sometimes high school, students. They may claim to be bored, but really doubt their own ability to read or understand the material correctly. Most do much better when they take classes in their twenties, thirties, or forties. By this time they have claimed their own mental authority and they feel more confident of their own learning and communication skills.

This is a rather dogged or stubborn mental placement. Learning becomes a means of gaining authority over your own life. Consequently that silent child, thought to be shy or dull, is thinking deeply of many things, often just waiting to put childhood behind.

## Saturn Conjunction the IC

Saturn is the foundation planet. This is more about authority than limits. It shows that your level of maturity has authorized this incarnation. In the third house, it is intended to give authority to your communication. In the fourth house it grants the right to self-supply . . . meaning that your level of financial and emotional security is self-generated. You bring emotional independence from past lives into this one.

## Saturn in the Fourth House

Family limits on feelings. This house placement initially overrides the sign placement, substituting family boundaries for personal boundaries. You may feel that your family and/or heritage limits you. You may prefer to remain childless because of it.

Your Authority Figure dominates your childhood. You may respect him or her. More often, you fear him or her. She or he limited your expression of feelings and often the supply of your needs. Sometimes this becomes a driving force to succeed, taken as a challenge from your Authority Figure and/or family.

Often the mark of abuse, this placement can refer to an undisciplined—meaning abusive—parent. You must constantly remain aware of your limits to feel safe at all. Consequently, you may seldom feel safe in such an environment. You may then grow up to feel unsafe when things get too calm, too peaceful. You may feel that you need some undisciplined person in your life, even when you know this is not true. A fourth house Saturn will probably get worked out in the seventh. The anger and/or fear engendered during your early years, must be dealt with in the significant-other relationships of your adult years. At some point, you must take back your authority, determining your own rights, rules, boundaries. You must reclaim ownership and control of your life.

## Saturn in the Fifth House

This posiiton limits our self-expression and creativity. Here your creativity is overruled by assigned duties. Your role in the family includes being responsible—probably responsible for the children. You are expected to act like an adult, and not a child. This differs from first house in that it may or may not be something you are equipped to do. First house *is* old for their age. Fifth house is expected *to act* older than their age, and may never learn to play.

This can have two results. You may continue to play the responsible parent role throughout life. Alternatively, you may complete your care-taking (parenting) duties while you are a child. You will then feel no need to become a parent by having your own children. This will free you to develop, to nurture, your creative talents. You will then have creations . . . as books, paintings, music, etc . . . instead of offspring.

Either way that you express this Saturn during your adult years, you will be quite serious about it. You can know that you are authorized to do the thing you enjoy, because it will seem more like play than work.

## Saturn in the Sixth House

This position teaches us that our usefulness is limited. This placement is often associated with depression because you can never feel useful enough. Whatever limits you seem to have on your health or your work come from a subliminal sense of uselessness during your early years. It really has no connection with your own abilities. Instead, you simply could not be used for the purpose that (at least one of) your parents intended.[9]

This usually manifests as one who works too hard, never being certain of what his or her physical limits are, or how much work is enough. Depression is usually rooted in frustration . . . the frustration of never feeling like anything is finished/enough. Physical health issues are rooted in overwork. Being sick is often the only recognizable permission to rest. Being sick enough or injured, may be the only recognizable permission to take life easier.

To heal this kind of soul-wound you must claim your authority to set your own boundaries on what is enough. Claim your authority to decide for yourself what your rightful duty is. Claim your right to use your life in some way that is less stressful, more pleasurable. Not all forms of usefulness need be *hard* work. Use your life for something that is easier on your body and your soul.

Saturn Conjunction the Descendant

This makes your Authority Figure your partner. It is as though you are married to him or her. You will need a divorce from this one before you can form any other successful partnerships. The Authority Figure forbids it—if not verbally, by taking up too much space in your life. Until you reclaim your authority, others will dominate your life, taking first place in all that you do. In the

---

[9]This is not about judging your parents. They were, after all, human. Perhaps they intended you to keep the marriage together or to be the family (son and) heir, etc.

Saturn in the Houses

sixth, it is because she or he uses your life as his or her own. In the seventh, the relationship is incestuous—sometimes sexually, always emotionally.

## Saturn in the Seventh House

This may limit your significant-other relationships, based on the notion that you lack self-discipline and/or responsibility. This does not preclude marriage or other unions, but does hinder the ability to attract a true equal. An unequal relationship can never be a valid marriage, nor can it be a true partnership.

Those you learn to call mates or partners do not mirror you. They may rule you, continuing the sabotage of your self-image begun by the adults in your childhood . . . because you gave them responsibility for your life. Here your authority figure opposes your self-image. She or he makes you not right and unequal.

With Saturn projected, you think of yourself as not-responsible because it is your only defense against abuse. Chances are the only thing for which you truly are not responsible is the treatment you receive. Meanwhile, your rights and your authority go unclaimed in the not-me house, until you notice and claim your maturity and independence. You must learn tough love. You must learn to set boundaries on what is acceptable treatment. You must demand respect.

> ### Setting Boundaries
>
> Visualize or affirm a circle drawn around yourself. Make it small at first if you need to, as you must be able to believe it exists. Inside that circle is your space and you make the rules. Choose what energies and experiences you will allow inside the circle and what you want kept out. *Example*: Only honest and trustworthy people can enter. This means that dishonest, untrustworthy people must change or leave. Always set the rules based on behavior, not individual people.
>
> The size of, and rules for, your circle can change at will, according to need and your comfort zone. You will find it much easier to keep unwanted experience out of your life than to learn how to deal with it once it gets in.

These are the prerequisites for happy and productive seventh house relationships—meaning all types of partnerships.

## Saturn in the Eighth House

In the eighth house, Saturn is not mine. Maturity, discipline, authority, rights and boundaries are forbidden, taboo, during childhood. More than that, the right to adulthood may also be denied, making a personal declaration of independence necessary at some pont in time.

This placement makes Saturn a dis-value, not-good for children. Here all rights, all authority, belong to adults, and you have no protection against what they do to you, because they invade your personal boundaries. Intending to contain you within their value system, Adults/Parents treat you as property rather than an individual with a right to your own life. They usurp the right to own and control you, and teach you to fear authority rather than to respect it.

In this house, Saturn can only represent an abusive Authority Figure, looming over your childhood. To stop the continuation of abuse, you must first claim your right to grow up, to individuate, to free yourself from parental law. Whatever self-discipline you learn must come from inside, or be learned from observation of the outside world. You must also build your own boundaries and defenses, taking back your right to do so from the adults who stole them. You have been treated as property. Transformation consists of taking back the ownership of, and right to, your own life.

## Saturn in the Ninth House

With this placement, the real authority is a spiritual one. However, initially, it is often understood to mean The Church. Usually, childhood is haunted by a vengeful god, administered by parents. This placement shows a type of atmosphere in which a child may be threatened with hellfire for the most minor infraction. Growing up with a terrible god, as abusive as the family authority figure, can drive the adult they become right out of a church that literally threatens death to their souls. Always, these natives must, at some point, define their own beliefs, independently of rigid parental belief systems.

This is an elevated position for Saturn, a place of honor and respect. Here discipline becomes discipleship, maturity is wise, and limits continually move outward as consciousness expands. Saturn in the ninth may be thought of as Divine Right. Spirit takes the form of Higher Mind. It grants the right to choose your own beliefs, make your own moral rules. It commonly confers a sense of being called, of being spiritually mature and meant to leave a mark on the world.

> ### Hidden Knowledge
>
> The eighth contains all the things which are not good for children to know ,have, etc. The house of hidden or occult knowledge, it may hide secrets about sex, death, and marital finances along with the truth about Santa Claus and the Easter Bunny.
>
> This is the house of *denial*, containing what we may not have . . . *until we reach maturity*.

At the same time, it may limit relationships, due to some spiritual belief, such as the idea of a celibate priesthood, and its permutations. Males may become sexually abstainate monks while females occasionally assume the mantle of temple prostitute.

Many natives are self-educated, as this Saturn sometimes limits the opportunities for formal higher education, while pouring much energy into some very serious spiritual studies that frequently lead to great wisdom.

## Saturn on the Midheaven

This draws your attention to issues like respect and reputation. Your goal may be influenced more by Saturn, than by the sign at the Midheaven. You may want to be an authority-in- your-field.

The true goal of this placement is to manage your life well. Doing so depends on your definition of authority–whether it is something to fear, or something to emulate. It may require you to overthrow the Authority of your childhood. Occasionally, if your idea of respect is fear, the goal will be about bossing others around! Beware of becoming the family autocrat!

## Saturn in the Tenth House

The tenth house is the maturity point. In a way, it represents what you expect to be when you grow up. It is closer to what you think that you should be, than to what you want to be. Saturn placed here may define you by your career and public image. By the same token, you may have a strong sense of this as something limited to a particular phase of your life. While the feeling of responsibility may be strong, it also has a definite endpoint, and natives may look forward to retirement. Tenth house Saturn is usually disciplined in traditional ways. They stay the course and are serious about their work. Consequently they often gain authority in later years of their career. Although this Saturn is usually successful in mundane terms, he will look forward to bringing career to a respectable conclusion.

The tenth house Saturn  may represent an Authority Figure who is highly respected, someone you look up to, a role-model for success. Alternatively, he or she will represent someone greatly feared, who hangs over your head. Largely depending on his sign placement, your authority figure will be a major help or a  hindrance to be overcome. Saturn nearly always has something to prove and the tenth house placement emphasizes that. Consequently, a threatening tenth house Saturn may drive you toward success. It is important that you take a good, honest look at your authority figure, and choose which elements are worthy of respect and emulation.

If you had a fear-based authority figure, you may redefine the very word authority. Autocracy is not authority, nor does it command respect. Respect is earned by a mature approach to life that includes common sense, wisdom, and emotional balance. The only inherent authority we have is the right to achieve management of our own lives. That authority is a side effect of maturity.  In the end, the real goal is to mature well, through self-discipline and independence. Doing so earns respect naturally.

## Saturn in the Eleventh House

The eleventh house is the "if I had a million dollars house," or it may be the "if I had time house." Placing Saturn there may initially seem to emphasize those limits. He may appear to stand in the way of your hopes and wishes, or keep you limited to hoping and wishing for what you never seriously believe that you can have.

However, the eleventh house holds a secret that will eventually overcome Saturn's apparent hindrances. It is the house of group or compounded consciousness. To make your wishes come true, it may be helpful to join with others who share your hopes.  Alternatively, the very compounding of energy that occurs when the same hopes and wishes are held over time, will, eventually break down the walls of resistance, and wishes will come true.

This is a good placement for a second career undertaken after official retirement. The eleventh always comes after the tenth. Saturn in the eleventh can bring success to a late-life, or second career.

For those with this natal position, we have a special recommendation. Imagine Saturn as a drawing pencil, a tool for drawing outlines of those things you hope or wish for. Daydream drawing pictures of what you want to acquire, do, or experience. When the outline is drawn, a void is created. Since the universe abhors a vacuum, it will fill in the outline and manifestation will occur. In this way, eleventh house Saturn can become a real friend, helping you to develop latent talent as an Adept.

## Saturn in the Twelfth House

This refers to unconscious, forgotten, or subliminal limits. Here you may feel limited without really knowing why. Such limits may have been set by forgotten early childhood trauma. Another possibility is repeated violation of your limits by one or more adults who behaved as though children have no personal boundaries. In modern times, another possible cause is derived from hospital treatment for birth issues like physical defects. A child who is hooked up to machines may have an unconscious memory of having its body invaded, and, as a consequence, never have learned to have conscious personal boundaries. Probably most common is the kind of limits absorbed from the environment. If adults behave as though they were limited, without ever speaking of it, the child may absorb the unconscious limits of the parents as natural and normal. It may take years of observation before you realize that such subliminal limits are not part of the human definition.

The good news about an unconscious Saturn is that by the nature of consciousness, what you do  not recognize cannot limit you. This is a prime placement for developing intuitive or artistic abilities because there are no human boundaries to tie your consciousness to the ground. Much will depend on Saturn's sign. Some signs are naturally more grounded than others. Saturn in an earth sign, for example, is far more likely to wake up than Saturn in water. Fire and air may go either way, depending on aspects.

# Saturn in the Signs

## Saturn in Aries

Saturn in Aries lives by the rules of survival, first of body, then of identity, finally of species. These rules outline the lives of natives. Some have survived in-utero attacks.

The first imperative is to survive long enough to grow up. Children born with this placement are often the targets of abusive, angry, authority figures. Many learn the art of invisibility, of avoiding notice by their abusers. Most grow up with some residual anger, because the abuse linked to the placement is usually battering.

The phrase banging your head against a wall may have first been used by a child, trying to find some way to please or appease an Aries authority figure. It simply cannot be done because the child is not the cause of such adult behavior. All too often the child is a lamb sacrificed on the altar of adult anger and/or dysfunction. Such children grow up in spite of their parents, not because of them. In such an atmosphere, all too often, hyper-vigilant reflexes linger far into adulthood. We may (be embarrassed to) find ourselves ducking, dodging and/or hiding from anyone who represents authority of any kind.

An even greater danger for the more evolved natives is that of conditioned expectation. If we cannot rid ourselves of the belief that we live in a dangerous world, we may attract or create danger. Others have developed habits of defensive aggression. These stand ready to fight, and doing so, attract the need to fight, to defend life, family, home and/or property.

Always, we must rid ourselves of deeply ingrained fear, disciplining ourselves to focus on the courage we have shown. From there, we must also search within for the origins of that courage.

Those origins must be faith, faith in their right to live, faith in their ability to pioneer new ways of being and doing. Somewhere within every native must lie the knowledge that we are, and have always been, survivors. Knowing that, we can know that no person can take life from us.

We can know that we have a divine right to live. When we really get that, we lose our fear, becoming fearless. We may then do what has not been done before, teach what has not been taught before. We have then been renamed. No longer Survivor, we become Pioneer and/or Seed Being.

### Saturn the Authority Figure

Aries Saturn usually describes a male authority figure. Always, the Authority Figure is the Head of Household. At best your authority figure is a Pioneer, one who models new ways of being and doing.

Far too often, Aries Saturn describes one who is angry and aggressive, violent and abusive. Such authorities may command fear, but never respect. This may leave you with little respect for authority figures. The placement pushes you to become your own authority, to find and/or create self-respect. Often this is rooted in acknowledging your courage.

### Saturn the Protector

This Saturn does not protect. You are your own protector. It is all up to you. The Saturn Figure is angry and probably paranoid. She or he may try to toughen you up through abusive treatment. More often, this person is so self-involved that s/he leaves you to your own devices. It is up to you to avoid their rage, along with all the normal pitfalls of childhood.

The great realization to be made is the recognition that you have parented yourself and been responsible for yourself from birth. This, of itself, should tell you that you are an evolved being.

Meanwhile, fear converts to anger, which converts to determination. Determination is established as a mental shout, "Thou shalt not!"

### Setting Boundaries

Visualize or affirm a circle drawn around yourself. Make it small at first if you need to, as you must be able to believe it exists. Inside that circle is your space and you make the rules. Choose what energies and experiences you will allow inside the circle and what you want kept out. *Example*: Only honest and trustworthy people can enter. This means that dishonest, untrustworthy people must change or leave. Always set the rules based on behavior, not individual people.

The size of, and rules for, your circle can change at will, according to need and your comfort zone. You will find it much easier to keep unwanted experience out of your life than to learn how to deal with it once it gets in.

### Personal Space and Boundaries

Personal boundaries are initially the skin, or just outside it. This means that we have no inviolable space beyond the limits of our body. For this reason, Aries Saturn may construct a hermit-like lifestyle, because the only way to have sufficient space for comfort is to avoid close relationships.

The lesson here is to redefine our sense of Self to include more than the body. If we make the size of our aura the limits of our space, we will have sufficient room to move about in society. We may even be able to form some comfortable relationships. The great lesson here is that definition of Self is the definition of boundaries. The only way to have more space is to have a greater sense of Self. This will include redefinition.

Saturn in the Signs

Personal limits are initially defined by our survival instincts. However, these are often confined to physical survival. At this level, we accept just about any behavior from others that is not life-threatening. We allow our lives to be harnessed, sacrificed to the needs of others, burglarized and generally abused, only defending ourselves when the situation becomes life- threatening. Much of our attention/energy is devoted to simply hanging on in untenable circumstances. We cannot grow while we stay within such limits.

At some point, natives must reclaim the right to posses and defend–not merely survival–but a truly desirable quality of life. Only then can we begin to acquire the substance necessary to add pleasure and beauty to our lives.

The only thing that truly limits Aries Saturn is lack of self-awareness—the awareness of our innocence. When we refuse to accept blame, or judgement from others, we are free to simply BE, as was intended. After that, we can begin to choose what/how we want to be.

**Personal Definition**

Personal definition involves how we describe ourselves. It is a primary aspect of Aries, whose key words are, "I am....." For Aries Saturn, a major life quest is "Who and/or What am I? Am I a higher animal? Am I a lesser god? Am I a synthesis of the two?"

Here the pioneer element may dominate. "Am I something new? Have I a new path, a new purpose? Am I the inception of a new version of humanity? Am I a Seed Being?"

Another side of this is "How am I? Am I impulsive? Am I original? Am I assertive, aggressive, angry? Am I ambitious? Am I a leader?"

All of these questions go into the creation of a personal definition and that definition also defines how much space you will need in order to express your beingness (your Sun).

Bible students may remember Genesis 10, in which Moses asked God for Its name. The answer was "I AM that I am." I am all that is. I am whatever I choose to be. This is the heritage to be remembered. As the Divine Parent is defined, so also should the divine offspring be defined. The lesser "I am" is potentially a mirror image, or genetic heir of the greater "I AM."

Conclusion: I am all that I choose to be. This is the only moral imperative for these natives. We must choose to be simply, clearly, without contamination, "I am".....whatever, whoever, however I choose to be.

**Discipline**

For Aries, this must always be self-discipline. The undisciplined adult can never teach discipline to a child. What you experienced as discipline during childhood was an expression of anger from your authority figure. You are left to make and enforce your own rules. As you define your own space and limits, you must have sufficient self-discipline to consider the consequences of your own actions and act within that context.

The consequences of an action by a child can be very different from the consequences of the same action by an adult. It may be safe to do now, what once would not have been safe during your earlier years.

## Responsibility

In some way your innocence has protected you and your survival instincts have found original ways to supply your survival needs. Still, your responses to your own needs may be quite primitive, and limited to mere physical survival. You do not let yourself starve for food, but you may allow other areas of your life to starve while doing so. As you once responded to your need to survive, you must now respond to your need for self expression and self worth

## Maturity

Aries is a new conception. It is the beginning of each new cycle of incarnation. Whatever maturity it has is a carry-over from earlier lifetimes. Maturity is, however, a potential implied in every seed, every inception, every conception. Maturity is then a natural consequence of living out the implications of the new cycle. For Aries Saturn, maturation consists of growing self-awareness.

## Rights and Authority

It is important to realize that, anything brand new, as Aries is, must also be innocent and uncontaminated. The rights of Aries Saturn are those conferred by innocence, purity, clarity.

They are the *rewards* earned in earlier incarnations. More than most, Aries Saturn must rely upon treasures laid up in Heaven for the freedom to express our full potential. Invested in Aries Saturn is the right to be all that you can be—and there is not much limit on that.

We are, then, our own authority. This may mean that we can violate certain socially accepted regulations, but the criterion for that will be our independence from society. Before we can do that, we must be physically, mentally, emotionally, and spiritually mature. Maturity is *always* the measure of authority. Maturity is our authorization for the full independence commonly considered an aspect of Aries.

## Saturn's Law

This is the absolute right to live, to be ourselves, to live by our own rules, our own inner guidance. We have the right to live free of criticism, judgment and/or condemnation. We are at the beginning of a new spiritual cycle, pioneering new territory. We are authorised to be unique, original, and independent of social demands. The only qualification for that, is that we must also grant those same rights to others.

# Saturn in Taurus

Saturn in Taurus lives by physical law. Whatever is physical has needs. It has to be fed. Formal structure has a magnetic charge designed to attract what is needed.

Saturn in Taurus is, then, a physical definition. It shows that our (view of) limits is a physical one. We regard ourselves as, or as contained within, a body. This should, automatically, attract physical health and possessions. When it does not, it is because a belief system denies the value of the body. The Earth experience has then lead to lowering of self-worth.

Under this placement, we first learn the value of self-worth. If we do not name ourselves good, we cannot attract good things. Then Saturn will represent a limit on what we can have.

Taurus Saturn describes a physical form of spirit. It is a particular and valuable phase of our spiritual development. The physical body grounds spirit into form. It outlines and defines a living spirit as a physical being. Perhaps the most important realization for natives is the fact that every entity has a body of some type. To make the journey through Earth incarnation, that body is created at a specific vibratory level.[10]

Metaphorically, we may say that incarnation requires a drop in level, to a rate that is perceptible to physical beings. If we are fallen at all, it is only a matter of slowing our atoms to a speed that is compatible with Earth habitation.[11] The value of taking physical form lies in that, for without a visible and tangible form, there is little spirit can accomplish on Earth.

Still, much of the religious world has insisted that a physical form is a hindrance to spirit, that spirit is somehow trapped in body, to be punished, to learn its lesson, to learn how to be good.[12] This leaves an aura of original sin and the result is a sense of never being good enough, and having no way to change that. It is Adam and Eve, kicked out of Eden, and left to earn their living in struggle and pain. Alternatively, from the East comes the idea of being caught on the wheel of Karma, struggling to earn our way back to Nirvana. Neither is punishment. Both ideas are misinterpretations, which deny the divine purpose for incarnating on Earth.

We are individual units of Spirit, in the process of self-discovery, self awareness. We are Deity getting to know itself as/in us. As Kryon says, "We are all pieces of God."[13]

Taurus is both fixed and earth, the most static of all the signs, the most limiting of Saturns.

---

[10]Think of this as atomic speed—the rapidity at which atoms move. For visibility on Earth, that must fall within a specific range. That speed-of-motion marks the difference between spirit-bodies and physical ones.

[11]Who knows? Perhaps the difference between human and angel is that some angels learn how to be psychically visible without dropping their consciousness level. Maybe they know how to transmit a self-image telepathically, so that we project it on our reality.

[12]In my client files, I could find only a few Taurus Saturn natives, all of whom were born in 1940-41 when Uranus was conjunct Saturn, allowing them to ignore their boundaries.

[13]From the Kryon series by Lee Carroll, available in bookstores, including Amazon.

When we believe that the body limits the spirit, it becomes a heavy weight, grounding it to Earth and the struggle for survival. Our Saturn boundaries are then like castle walls, which although built to keep evil out, trap us inside. The great lesson for Taurus Saturn is to realize the true value of incarnation as a phase in the development of self-awareness. Earth is a learning environment. It is where we step away from our divinity long enough to ground it in reality and make it conscious. It is but a step on the path to god-consciousness.

## Saturn the Authority Figure

The Taurus Authority Figure is possessive. She or he administers discipline for your own good, and you get a lot of instruction about how to be good. A close examination may show that it is more about getting you to conform to what makes the parent look good.

The Taurus Authority Figure is more owner than a parent. They manage your life as though it were their property. You are expected to stay in your proper place, to behave according to their definition of my child. Most of these Authority Figures want a yes person, not a living, growing, learning, child. They want your behavior to be a credit to their training. The result is that most natives grow up well-trained in the art of people-pleasing.

Consequently, many natives grow up with their security invested in belonging to another. Because Taurus Saturn conditioning is so deep, it takes great strength of will to retake ownership of your own soul, your own life. You are taught to always be good, meaning obedient and compliant in order to avoid upsetting others. Under such restraints, making any changes in the status quo can be difficult and upsetting. Sometimes it even feels life-threatening, as though you could not survive without the security of being family/parental property. Consequently, it is very difficult to expand your horizons, because you are conditioned to limitation, as though tethered to another person's needs, power, or will.

## Saturn the Protector

This Saturn is not very protective, because his protection is conditional. It depends on meeting standards of appearance and/or behavior, as defined by your Authority Figure. You are required to be worth protecting, to be a personal asset to your protector.

As with Aries, you need to realize that you have always been your own protector. The way you protected yourself was by submission, and you did it under threat of being left unprotected, uncared for. There is always an element of caste in the family of natives, as though one must be good enough to be kept. You know that property which does not meet parental standards gets replaced, and some natives struggle with the fear that they may be replaced in their families.

With Saturn in Taurus, there is always a sense of having to earn your place and your protection. You have to be good enough to measure up to family standards. You must make your family/parents look good. It can be more important to have good manners and a pleasing appearance than it is to be honest.

The great gift of this Saturn is that it quite naturally values life. Because it does, it automatically acts to protect itself, investing life in its own physical care and protection. Natives do what is required to assure that physical needs are met. Initially that will be food, as an energy source. Later it will be money, because money is the energy on which society runs. All too often, how much food or money that you have becomes the limit on your life.

This pattern may be reinforced by adults who condition their children by offering rewards of food and/or money. Some parents maintain control of their young adult children, by keeping them dependant on money from home. The subtle underlying message is that the price of your life is your spirit/identity. The price you pay for parental assistance can be much too high. The only thing between you and abundant good is low self-worth.

For many, the first step in overcoming that, is reversal. Spiritual growth then comes at the price of living in poverty, so the boundaries remain in place until you realize that you are, you were always, good enough. There is no standard of goodness between you and the spirit of love and provision.

Healing comes through integrating spirit, soul and body. Integration comes through the realization that body is merely a form of spirit. There is no more innate difference between body, soul and spirit than there is between ice, water and steam. That is the valuable lesson awaiting every Taurus Saturn. Knowing that, the value of your life can never again be limited by Saturn, or by anything else. You will then own your own life and you will have access to all that you need or want.

**Personal Space and Boundaries**

Taurus outlines are constructed of physical possessions. The primary possession is the body. Above all it needs to be owned and valued by the native. Until it is, you will be subject to the will of others, and they will own your life.

When you are defined as a possession, you get only as much space as you physically occupy. If you do not retain your value, you will no longer have that. Consequently, hanging onto the space that you have, becomes a primary goal. This can limit spiritual growth to the dimensions of the body. Sometimes it leads to obesity, as the spirit attempts to expand its boundaries. While you define yourself as a body, it must remain inside the body and the only way to grow is to expand the body.

While your life is defined in terms of possession, should you escape possession, you may begin accumulating possessions as a defense against being repossessed. This is another form of obesity, where your life becomes encumbered by the accumulation of things. The need to retain a weighty body or lifestyle is a physical expression of the survival instinct. The apparent greed of some Taurus Saturns is a thin veneer over the fear of death–not merely physical death, but spiritual death.

To have more space in your life requires you to redefine your outlines. See yourself as more than a body. Realize that your body may be temporary, but your life is not. Envision an aura of whatever size you wish. Repeat and repeat, until you begin to feel more in touch with your own soul and spirit, until your life begins to be more pleasurable. Realize that you have a magnetic field (of influence) and that, as you name your self "good," you attract good things.

When fear comes up, turn your attention to cataloging all your positive assets and qualities. Keep your eyes on the good. Speak appreciation and praise. These are the attractors of greater good.

## Personal Definition

Personal definition involves how we describe ourselves. Taurus Saturn often bypasses the "I am" and goes directly to "I have," defining themselves by their possessions, acquisitions and assets. A big issue is always, "What is my body (or my life) good for? What do I do well?"

Since acquisition is a large issue, it is important to examine the accumulation of things in your life. Ask of each, "what is this good for now?" Most things and relationships that are not producing something of value in the present should be let go. This allows space for the entry of greater good. It has been said that you cannot receive present gifts if your hands are full of the past. Remember this.

Saturn is a defining element. It shows how we are intended to define or name our lives. Saturn in Taurus *must* name life good. Saturn by any other name will outline our lives according to that name.

Life is good and it will remain good unless we name it otherwise. How foolish it is to name a particular form of life not good, or less than. It is no more appropriate than to say that oxygen is not-good when it is concentrated into a solid.

A keyword for Taurus is "good." Know then, that an important task for every Taurus Saturn is to replace every not-good in your life with good. You were born a good person, naturally good, naturally valuable. Taurus is the very spirit of goodness and the Saturn placement is your definition. Even the limits you encounter are good, being for your good, or good for something. Upon you encountering any person, force or event, ask this: "What is this good for?" Keep your focus on looking for the good in all things and your life will become increasingly pleasant.

## Discipline

As a child, most of what passed for discipline was coercion. Some adults, regarding you as property, bent you to their will. Often you were coerced into staying within their limits–many of which were obsolete and/or irrelevant to your life. "I do this for your own good." may have been a common theme. As an adult, you may have to peel off layers of this conditioning to discover what truly is for your own good.

Natives are often called stubborn. Adults attempt to break their will. It is important to examine that. Was your stubbornness resistance to having your personality shaped for the pleasure or comfort of others? If so, then you were stubbornly hanging on to the very essence of you. Let no person judge that, least of all you! Notice that stubborn people are those who hang in there, who see things through to conclusion. They never give up. They finish things. Stubbornness may be your best quality, not your worst.

As an adult, your greatest disciplinary challenge will be that of recovering and nurturing your self worth. Discipline yourself to remember that you are, naturally and innately good, that you are valuable in the greater plan for life. You do not have to prove your worth. *You are worthy of all good things.*

## Responsibilities

Taurus is the sign of integrity. We may think of Taurus Saturn as structural integrity.[14]

Integrity is another term often misused. Ultimately, it refers to holding things together with a magnetic charge. Metaphysics expresses this as like attracts like. Often called the principle of love, it is really the principle of magnetics. As love attracts love, hate attracts hate. The creative attractor is attention, so whatever we focus our attentions upon will attract more of the same type of attention. Here is the crux of the problem and the gift.

If we call our limits good/Taurus, they will serve us well. If we call them not-good/Scorpio, they will bring only harm. So the great responsibility of Taurus Saturn is to find the value of limits. That value is the protection that is offered to a growing child, first a physical child, later a spiritual child. Above all, it points to the value of embodiment as a spiritual process.

The body concentrates spiritual energy into a physical form, for a specific purpose. That is its value. It is our responsibility to discover that, to realize its value, and to affirm that value. *It is not about becoming good. It is about seeing the good already present.* As we do so, the natural magnetic process will add more value to the outlines of our life. It will be not so much about becoming bigger, as becoming richer.

## Maturity

Taurus is a new embodiment. Thus, the body may be experienced as a limit on a spirit accustomed to greater freedom. Maturation will be the acceptance of the body. It will include learning to trust the body. True maturity will be the reevaluation of the body as a wonderful vehicle in which the spirit travels. There are many things which spirit may only learn, do, be in physical form. When we recognize the true value of physical experience, we are truly mature.

For Taurus Saturn, maturation consists of growing self-acceptance and appreciation for the physical experience.

## Authority and Rights

Taurus Saturn focuses our attention on (portable) possessions, most often money or other expressions of concrete value. We are authorized to have as much as we name rightfully ours. To do so, we must focus on our innate goodness, realizing that by birth, we are worthy. Taurus Saturn

---

[14] A term borrowed from the television series of spaceships—Enterprise, Voyager, etc.

describes a valuable form of life, which based on its magnetic aspect, is authorized to manifest all good things by right of its divinely beloved form.

Attention defines or outlines our life. If we perceive Saturn as a hindrance, rather than a simple outline or horizon, we will limit the flow of good into our lives. This Saturn is authorized to create or generate wealth, in all its forms. That wealth will manifest as tangible goods.

It is authorized to prove the value of a human life, lived as a form of spirit. Spirit is the substance of physical form. We may say that it is elemental life. Like any element, spirit may change its form, but not its nature.

When you chose, or were given, a Taurus Saturn, you were authorized to claim all spiritual rights while in physical form. It was not an easy assignment, because most of the world would deny you those rights. Still, by the very power of God/dess, you are authorized to name all things good, and by that naming, to reintegrate them into the goodness of spirit. In so doing, you reinforce the structural integrity of Life.

All it requires is to reclaim your authority, the authority to reiterate the Creator's command from Genesis. Look on life and see that all is good, if only that it is all good for something. This is the essence of faith and trust, that we believe that it is all good, no matter what we have been led to think, no matter how it looks.

### Saturn's Law

This is the absolute right to take pleasure in our own lives, by living life as we (our spiritual beingness) created it. It is the right to have all that we need or desire, even all that we hope, wish, or dream. It is our decree of worthiness. We are authorised to formulate our own destiny, to shape our lives as we will. *The only qualification for this is that we must also grant those same rights to others.*

# Saturn in Gemini

Saturn in Gemini defines/outlines us as a conscious being, capable of data collection <u>and</u> communication. It may also describe mental limits, a limit on available data, a limit on verbal expression, and/or proscribed thinking, speaking, and/or questioning. It implies that mind is limited by or to logic. This comes from the fact that logic is dual by nature, being a process of classification based on contrast or comparison. We learn a variety of either-or classifications, such as life is light or dark, good or bad, useful or useless, creative or destructive. Gemini functions from true-and-false, not yet realizing that life is multiple choice.

When Saturn is in Gemini, we are defined by the way we name ourselves, and especially the way we name our Mercury mind. The only thing that really limits our lives, and the appearance of our intelligence, is that we are faced with too many conditioned boundaries. This amounts to a kind of mental double-vision. What we can learn is initially limited by conditioning that sets up double standards of thought and/or behavior. Double or multiple files fill up memory, limiting the ability to add new information to our personal data base. This can be done in several ways.

Later in life, natives may be caught in the repeating pattern of attempting to choose between two kinds of boundaries. Mundanely, the choice is between what you can do and what you should do. The discussion or argument quite naturally limits how far you can go, in space or consciousness. Consequently, Gemini Saturn seems to block your perceptions, by keeping you too busy, handling too much data, to move to a place of wider perspective. The short journeys of Gemini initially refer to a lack of perspective. They keep us too close to see clearly. We begin life in a nearsighted way and can only improve our distance vision by expanding our original boundaries. To do so, we learn to ask the unasked questions, to seek within for answers withheld by others.

This Saturn can be a voice in your ear, whispering caution. He can also foster a constant ongoing internal argument. It is like trying to manage by committee. Every member has a different idea, and they seldom agree. . . . Focus is disrupted by information overload.

This can manifest as a learning disability. It sometimes takes the form of the double vision or garbled sound reception, called dyslexia. Usually regarded as a physical condition, dyslexia emerges from or correlates to a psychological one. It is easier for adults to think of children as ill or handicapped than to accept responsibility for the conditioning which always underlies these problems.

## Saturn the Authority Figure

Our Authority Figure establishes both the rules of behavior, and the rules about how life works. Hopefully, they will agree, at least in principle. A good Authority Figure sets a good example of responsible behavior, modeling an effective way to live.

One Saturn lesson is critical, especially for Gemini Saturn. Discipline cannot be learned from an undisciplined adult. Abusers are not true authorities. They are, instead, power figures who control with fear. If you are afraid of your authority figure, s/he is an abuser who substitutes might for right.

Saturn in Gemini can show two (or more) Authority Figures, each with their own set of rules. Today's classic example is the child whose parents share custody. Each household has its own rules and its own authority figure and the child must keep them straight.

Occasionally, parents of differing religions and/or cultures set up similar double standards within one household. The young native must remain focused on which person is managing which portion of his or her childhood.

Alternatively and historically, Gemini is a split Authority Figure—commonly an alcoholic, rage addict, or one with some other illness, which requires you to know how far you can go according to the mental/emotional condition of the authority. Rules may change drastically depending how this person feels. Notice that in such situations, both parents are affected, as the enabling parent will attempt to enforce whatever changing rules the addict has in effect at the moment. You may then lose respect for both, resulting in a lack of respect for authority.

Or you may simply fear authority, because your reactions were conditioned by irrational authority figures.

Life is particularly difficult when natives must learn and live by two different sets of rules. The child is required to maintain two memory files for everything. We have doubled belief and/or value systems. This can be very confusing, and completely disrupts reactions and responses. These functions cannot become automatic because there must always be a pause to select the proper memory file. Sometimes this leads to confusion over right and left because what is right in one case is wrong in another.

It can also set up a barrier between right and left brain, so that we must choose the logical way or the intuitive way. Your mind can be so overworked dealing with reality that there is no room for developing the imagination. When one must constantly make survival-based choices,

the ability to extend or expand awareness into other realms is curbed. This placement is not about limited intelligence. It is about hindered or blocked intelligence.

Within this framework, we may also include the Authority Figure who uses the do what I say, not what I do approach. This sets up another type of double standard, particularly in the area of how life works. Much confusion can arise from watching parents who claim that success comes from one set of behaviors, while they live a very different one. This can set us up for

failure, because our automatic responses are governed by what our parents modeled, while our thinking is governed by what they said.

Often, when you begin to move on instinct, your mind argues, and the result is no action. This is the root of much that gets named procrastination. However you try to move, one boundary or another trips you. You must first choose between your Authority Figures, and that throws you back into the feelings of a childhood where nothing was certain. The only solution is to take back your authority from them both.

**Saturn the Protector**

No adult really protects these natives. With the split Saturn, one parent may teach avoidance techniques, but these are simply methods of protecting yourself. Sometimes Gemini Saturn gets some protection from an older sibling, but only as the sibling is accepted as yet another Authority Figure.

This placement can also refer to the joint protection offered by a group of siblings who conspire together to avoid fearful behaviors of adult Authority Figures.

Real protection comes from developing a set of automatic responses to danger, such as the flinch response that pulls a hand away from a hot stove. However, with too many Authority Figures, responses can never become automatic or instinctive. A delay is inserted, while we sort through multiple response options.

Wherever we find Gemini, there is often much mental static—too many voices in your head, often arguing with each other. One of the most effective protections for this is to talk steadily, or create some other white noise. If you cannot find some method of dealing with Saturn double-talk, you may stop listening to yourself at all. When you do that, you have lost your own voice, your own authority.

In the end, this placement requires us to define our own boundaries, for ourselves. First, realize that you are your own authority, your own protector. Then discipline yourself to serious affirmative work. This can overwrite all the voices in your head.

## Personal Space and Boundaries

Initially, Gemini Saturn sets up dual (sometimes multiple) space boundaries. You are required to remember a variety of safe distances, based on place, time, person, or other qualifications. It may be safe to cuddle with Authority Figures in one context and safer to run or hide in another. Sometimes it is safer to be close to strangers than family, or vice versa. It comes back to the same problem. Saturn limits your thinking by keeping your mind constantly engaged in sorting for safety.

This can leave you with a poor understanding of personal space that leaves you open to invasion by others. Alternatively, you may not recognize the boundaries others have. Not knowing how close is close enough can become very destructive to the art of forming relationships.

Begin by forming a relationship with yourself, finding your voice beneath all the parental voices in your head. In the end, this boundary between you and others can be your salvation, because you <u>must</u> first find your own identity, your own voice. Once you know who you are, and can hear your own guidance, the space issue will resolve itself. Your automatic responses will be free to work for you.

> ## Setting Boundaries
>
> Visualize or affirm a circle drawn around yourself. Make it small at first if you need to, as you must be able to believe it exists. Inside that circle is your space and you make the rules. Choose what energies and experiences you will allow inside the circle and what you want kept out. Example: Only honest and trustworthy people can enter. This means that dishonest, untrustworthy people must change or leave. Always set the rules based on behavior, not individual people.
>
> The size of, and rules for, your circle can change at will, according to need and your comfort zone. You will find it much easier to keep unwanted experience out of your life than to learn how to deal with it once it gets in.

## Personal Definition

Personal definition involves how we describe ourselves. Saturn in Gemini may define the self according to perceived intelligence, often as compared to a sibling. Thinking of yourself as less intelligent than another may discourage you from developing your own abilities. Thinking of yourself as more intelligent, can load you with responsibilities, on the grounds that you can do more than others, and because you can you are obligated to do so. Either way, your intelligence becomes a restriction on your life, one that blocks naturally developing self-awareness.

Often, what lies behind this labeling is two siblings who may be equally intelligent, but have different information processing styles. One may be left-brain dominant—a (usually) right- handed person whose style is logical. The other may be right-brain dominant (usually left-handed and/ or left-eyed) with an intuitive/artistic style. In such an event, they simply mirror the pillars of the Gemini symbol (II), which represents one mind with two united functions.

## Responsibility

Initially, we learn that it is our responsibility to memorize all the multiple rules and behaviors required to live with people who are bigger and stronger than we are. There may seem to be no set right and wrong ways to be or do. This can arrest our maturation process. When the mind is confined by overwork, it can keep us dependant on others for far too long. In the end, it is always our responsibility to reclaim our authority and to choose our own limits and boundaries.

Gemini is the origin of Magic and Scientific prayer, the place where we first confront the power in names and words. The great lesson of Gemini Saturn is that we must name our own boundaries and define our own limits. If we say that we cannot learn because of some physical disability, we make it so on both ends. It reinforces the learning problems and creates or adds to the disability. Equally, if we learn focus, by excluding irrelevance, if we learn to silence the nagging of internal false authority, we may heal our lives. Let Gemini Saturn redefine us as highly intelligent and conscious beings. *The more we say it, the more we make it so.*

## Maturity

Gemini refers to new awareness, or awareness functioning at a new level. It is learning as a maturation process. Because it is young-in-phase, it is learning to communicate, to express its intelligence in words. Ultimately it is about learning a language in which to think, communicate, and with which to relate.

When Saturn is in Gemini, our personal boundaries are created by and from the words we use. The more we speak from the innocence of youth, the better our lives work. Only as we learn to lie, criticize and judge, do we create blockages to our natural creativity. Children learn these from adults. They are not the natural state. It behooves Gemini Saturn to reclaim its innocence, to speak boundaries that protect us from judgement, criticism and/or condemnation. If we insist on our youthful innocence, we free the creative inner child.

Interestingly, this placement suggests that maturity consists of staying in the moment, refusing the influence of past failures and future fears. In this moment, we know what to do, how to be. In this moment, we are eternally young, eternally growing, eternally learning.

When we live from this eternal stance, maturity becomes irrelevant, because time no longer exists. We are what we are, what we have always been, what we will always be.

**Rights and Authority**

More than most, Gemini Saturn must and can name it and claim it. The first step in the process is to redefine ourselves as independent adults, with the rights and the authority to choose our own lifestyle, beliefs, and moral values. We have the right to protect ourselves, and to manage our lives as we see fit.

First, become your own teacher. If that seems too large a task, find a teacher whose teachings about life and morality are rational. This means *one teacher*, not two or three. Your most important lesson in life is the disciplining of your own mind. You must teach it to listen to only one voice. If the voice is not yours at first, it must become yours. Affirm, affirm, and affirm, rewriting the old tapes.

Second, exercise discipline by refusing to allow your mind to argue with itself. The simple method is to change the subject. We all have ways that engage our minds sufficiently to give them a rest. For some, inane television programs or romance novels work best. For others, it might be exercise, music or some creative project. It matters not what you use. *It matters only that you use it.*

The key is not to try to stop the mind chatter, but rather to refuse it the time, space and energy it has been using. It is a habit and can be retrained.

Draw a mental picture of yourself that comes from your innate sense of self, one that excludes all opinions but your own. The more clearly you envision your own outlines, the more successful your life will become.

Little by little, you become your own voice of authority, maturing into a highly intelligent being, albeit often a late bloomer. Gradually, learn to attune to the intuitive first answer or choice, refusing to argue yourself out of it. In the end, the most logical choice is, always and forever, the intuitive one. It is the sum of all the logical processing you have done in past incarnations.

The eventual intent of this placement is that we should learn to use our Mercury-mind to tune in to the vast Neptunian realm. In this way the duality of Gemini is resolved, but for most, this will come later in the evolutionary journey. For most, Saturn in Gemini simply refers to conditioning that clogs the mental processes with too much data. Too much data comes from too many instructions and too many authorities. You have learned that life was a choice, that you must choose between them. It was a lie. Let Neptune erase old boundaries. Let Uranus break old rules. Claim the Power of Pluto and the Authority of Saturn to rule your own life.

Be true to yourself, speak from your own knowledge, live your own truth. A good way to do that is to live in the moment. If you stay in the present, the voices of the past must fade away.

If you wish, you may let them have authority over the past, but they have none in the present, none in the future. Today is yours. You have every right to it.

### Saturn's Law

Saturn's law is the law of naming. Gemini Saturn grants the right to name life as we will. Like Adam in Eden, all that we perceive is ours to name, so name it good. The great lesson of our lives is that of learning to name ourselves and all else according to its original goodness. What we name good will attract goodness. What we name bad will attract evil. Saturn's lesson and law is as simple as that.

We have the absolute right to think for ourselves, to choose our own limits, to speak our own ideas. Since we define ourselves by our intelligence, we must name ourselves intelligent. We must set no limits on how intelligent we are or how much we can learn. There are none.

We are authorized to learn as much as we desire, in the style that is most comfortable. *The only qualification for that, is that we must grant equal rights to others.*

# Saturn in Cancer

Saturn in Cancer defines us in terms of our birth. In a sense, we keep the feeling of being bounded by the womb from which we emerged longer than other Saturns do. In practice, it suggests that our boundaries are not our own, that we still live within the confines of those limits which outlined the life of our Mother.

We feel limited by our feelings, or by our Mother, our childhood, or our family. To *feel* limited does not mean that we *are* limited. Cancer is a sign of growth. Our boundaries are meant to grow. We are designed to outgrow our original limits.

To understand this Saturn, it is necessary to understand that feelings are the mind of the body. (See box.) Their purpose is to tell us what we need. Feelings are limited to the basics: hunger, thirst, pleasure, pain. Although we may confuse feelings and emotions, they are not the same. Emotions are outward motions that show a reaction to feelings—the reaching for food, drink, pleasure and/ or the drawing back from pain.

Ultimately, this placement refers to a feeling structure that remains immature beyond the normal time of development. This occurs because we have insufficient exposure to people other than Mother during our developmental phase. She holds us too close preventing our maturation into emotionally independent beings.. Our boundaries may remain childish overlong,showing delayed maturation. This is the mark of the late bloomer. Still, if we bloom late, we may live extra years as needed to fulfill our pre-incarnational intent.

### Saturn the Authority Figure

Our Authority Figure establishes both the rules of behavior, and the rules about how life works. Hopefully, they will agree, at least in principle. A good Authority Figure sets a good example of responsible behavior, modeling an effective way to live.

Saturn in Cancer is really an antithesis or oxymoron. The authority figure may feel responsible

### Feelings—Mind and Body

Feelings are the mind of the body. They tell us what we need by registering hunger, thirst, pleasure, pain, etc. The way we learn to recognize and respond to feelings differs widely from the way we learn to walk and talk. It is the purpose for which the mother-child bond was created.

During the period while our mother carries us in her body and in her arms, mother and child share feelings. They are undifferentiated and we do not know that we are a person separate from her. This allows us to learn how to recognize and respond to our feelings by experiencing how she recognizes and responds to her feelings and needs. At the same time, she registers our feelings and needs as her own, allowing her to understand what her child needs during the period prior to language development.

It is important to realize that whatever is absorbed pre- verbally will set up an automatic response system. That is the importance of the emotional system. It is a part of consciousness that can respond automatically, without the process necessary to thought. Example: If you touch the stove, you do not have to think about the threat involved or what to do about it. Your hand jerks away automatically. Much of what we do impulsively comes from such an automatic response. Very often it has little to do with our real needs or desires. Instead it belongs to our mother.

When our development proceeds in the currently prescribed manner, sometime during the first year or so of our lives, we establish a second bond with our father. Doing so allows us to become aware that people have differing needs. Gradually, we are exposed to more people. Out of that experience, we learn to sort out our needs from those of the people around us. At this point we

begin to separate and individuate. When the process malfunctions, we grow up with difficulties based on poor boundaries and/or a poor sense of identity, low self-image, self-worth, etc. All too often we spend years pursuing the satisfaction of needs or desires that have no relevance to our true/spiritual Self.

*And then there are the Indigos and Crystals* who, in this sense, do not have a mother-child bond, *because they do not need one.* They have evolved to a point where they can retain their established need system—presumably from prior incarnations.

for children, but not authorized to make any rules or set any boundaries.

The Cancer Authority Figure is (usually) Mother, and she is more a caretaker than an authority. Often she is dependant, with no real authority of her own. Discipline may be deferred as, "Wait until your father gets home." During your school years, she may fight with us more than disciplining us. Often she was a victim of childhood abuse and is afraid to discipline her children for fear of becoming abusive.

With a dependant Saturn sign, we may feel that success requires dependency. Your success will then depend on others and will be secondary to theirs. You may have a successful spouse and your public image will depend on his reputation. Remember: You are authorized to outgrow this dependency, to grow into a strong independant being. Cancer is, after all, a cardinal sign, so the growth is toward independence.

### Saturn the Protector

Cancer Saturn is far more protector than authority. Usually, Mother is the protector. Often she stands between you and the family disciplinarian. The disciplinarian may be childish or narcissistic, a grandiose personality who expresses feelings in abusive ways. Note: Abuse is not consistently negative behavior. It *is inconsistent behavior* that prevents you from anticipating consequences relative to the abuser.

This placement can make it difficult to leave home. You may only feel safe with Mother nearby. You depend on her for safety. It is important to realize that this type of protection is rather shallow. Whenever anyone is threatened by the negative emotions of another, a parent is obligated to separate their child/ren from that person. Only in that way, can soul wounds be prevented. Be aware that you may be limited by old feelings of fear and/or anger—feelings repressed so that the anger condenses into boundaries. You may need professional help in releasing these.

Growing up with an abusive adult creates scars, even if you are not the target of the abuse. It grooves your soul to habitual responses that transfer the threat of abuse to other adults, males, etc. That which you fear you are likely to attract, and in doing so, pass on the abusive pattern to yet another generation.

> ## Setting Boundaries
>
> Visualize or affirm a circle drawn around yourself. Make it small at first if you need to, as you must be able to believe it exists. Inside that circle is your space and you make the rules. Choose what energies and experiences you will allow inside the circle and what you want kept out. Examle: Only honest and trustworthy people can enter. This means that
>
> dishonest, untrustworthy people must change or leave. Always set the rules based on behavior, not individual people.
>
> The size of, and rules for, your circle can change at will, according to need and your comfort zone. You will find it much easier to keep unwanted experience out of your life than to learn how to deal with it once it gets in.

In he end you must create our own protection by learning to set boundaries against those who would threaten your emotional and/or physical security.

Another idea is to get in touch with your angels, even if you have to imagine them at first. We do have guardian angels, even if they look like our mother or some other person. Trust yours or trust yourself to stay out of unsafe relationships.

Growing up with an abusive adult creates scars, even if you are not the target of the abuse. It grooves your soul to habitual responses that transfer the threat of abuse to other adults/males/ etc. That which you fear, you are likely to attract, and doing so, pass on the abusive pattern to yet another generation.

In the end, you must create your own protection, by learning to set boundaries against those who would threaten your emotional and/or physical security.

Another idea is to get in touch with your angels–even if you have to imagine them at first. We do have guardian angels, even if they look like our mother or some other person. Trust yours, or trust yourself to stay out of unsafe relationships.

## Personal Space and Boundaries

With Cancer Saturn our personal space and its boundaries are fluid and changeable. They are conditional, depending on the circumstances or the persons present. It can feel like our relationships cramp our style, if we have unaddressed feelings toward others—even/especially, when these are projected.

Combining Cancer and Saturn, ruler of Capricorn usually points to a parental issue. When parental issues are present, they shape our significant-other relationships. This can make us feel responsible for all the feelings around us and/or we find ourselves feeling the feelings of others as our own. Either way, we will feel defensive and respond to others accordingly.

The key difficulty here is our conditioning toward depending on others to define us. If we are willing to outgrow that, we may then set personal boundaries more in keeping with our own beingness (Sun sign).

## Personal Definition

Personal definition involves how we describe ourselves. Saturn in Cancer may define the self according to needs, or as dependant. Here the condition to life is the need for growth and maturation. This is not different from everyone else, but is emphasized with Cancer Saturn. It suggests that we respond to life from a focus of what we need from it. This may be expressed as: "I am the person who cannot_____because I lack something that I need." In fact, all that is ever needed is maturation.

In effect, the personal definition is that of "child." The complication in this comes from a traditional attitude which classifies mothers and their children as a group that is dependant on the father or head of household. Cancer Saturn segregates us from the big people with the big voices on whom we depend for our definition. We may then be just one of the needy people who depend on this person.

Alternatively, we may define ourselves as emotional. This usually has some degree of negativity attached to it. In fact, it suggests that our limits are attached to or created by our Moon. The Moon initially represents our mother, but should evolve into our Soul. The Soul is the channel or format for Solar energy, shaping it to our chosen work/service.

The result of understanding this is that our incarnational-intent outlines and defines our lives. We will then define ourselves in terms of our purpose in life.

Now notice that growth is a purpose for every life. With this placement, we <u>intend</u> to grow into our chosen task and/or role.

### Responsibility

Because of the Cancer-Capricorn effect, we may take responsibility for others before, or instead of, ourselves. We may use issues of (emotional)dependency and (financial)responsibility to define our lives.As we had difficulty leaving home, we may also have difficulty letting our children learn responsibility, especially as it involves leaving home.

It is critical that we realize that allowing our children to gradually assume responsibility for themselves is our primary responsibility to them. We must let them, help them, to grow up into independent adults who take responsibility for themselves and their own actions.

Because of this, some natives delay or even abstain from parenting. Let there be no criticism of that!

### Mauurity

With Saturn in Cancer, maturation is often out of sync with the actual age. Sometimes children are old for their age. Later they may become rather childish adults for a while. Usually this will be outgrown. Cancer Saturn can produce a youthful attitude in people of advancing years. Keep in mind that anything in Cancer is designed to grow continuously into ever-maturing manifestation. In some, a peak is reached, followed by a rebirth and a new growth cycle.

Initially, it is our responsibility to feel—to take care of—the feelings of those around us. Realistically, our safety often depends on it. Later, we must find ways to adapt that ability to adult life. We must realize that we are not children. In some way, we are responsible for our own maturation, but much of that depends on reconditioning our feeling structure, and re-parenting ourselves. This is about facing our conditioned fears and getting beyond them. It is about realizing that we are now as big as the big-people who once made us feel unsafe.

### Rights and Authority

Ultimately, Saturn in Cancer confers the right to grow, to remain youthful, to tend our own growing boundaries. Because we have had little true discipline during our developmental years, we are forever subject to growing levels of self-discipline. We are required to make and apply our own rules, to change them as needed, and to keep on growing. Early in life, this kind of growth may have been inhibited by circumstances, but it was always latent.

It may be important to note that Saturn rules the skin. We do grow our own skin and it continues to grow, at first larger—to house a larger skeletal structure—then to replace and renew aging skin. It conforms to the needs of a maturing body.

Even as you have the right and the authorization—by virtue of being alive—to grow your own skin, so you have the right and the authority to grow/expand your aura as your soul matures. It is largely a natural process that requires little attention beyond the recognition that you have grown beyond the conditions—and consequent needs—of childhood. Having survived that childhood is your authorization to claim the rights of a spiritually mature being.

## Saturn's Law

Saturn's law is the law of growth, and of eternal life. It is significant that, in the natural chart, Cancer is at the base. This shows that growth is a prerequisite for life. *Life is that which grows, changes, becomes.* Life is that which is born, grows to its limits, and then reborn in a new form.

Eternal life is founded on this. So long as we are growing, we are alive. Generally, growth begins with the physical, then is focused into the social, and finally into the spiritual. Still, there are many ways to grow. We think of a statement about the young Jesus-ben-Joseph. It was said that he grew "in wisdom, and in stature, and in favor with God and man." If we choose the path of continued growth, we extend life. If we choose to stop growing, we may end one cycle to be reborn in another. Whether on Earth or elsewhere, we are designed to be born and reborn, time after time. Whether on Earth or elsewhere, life is eternal. In one way or another, this law applies to all. It is automatic. There are no conditions.

# Saturn in Leo

With this placement, we are limited by our heritage or family reputation. This is particularly true when children grow up in the same small town where one or both parents grew up. You will then inherit expectations based on your family name. If parents, grandparents, etc. were wild, intellectually slow, social misfits, etc., you may be unfairly limited by the social stigma earned by earlier generations. Positive reputations also get projected and you may be faced with unreasonable expectations, or coerced into a role unsuitable to your being structure.

Another aspect of this placement is that of being limited by your talents. Talents you do not think that you have may hinder action. Talents of which you are aware may have conditioning attached that makes them burdensome, as the child star who is expected to support the family reputation and/or provide for them financially.

This Saturn could be quite spiritual, but at this time, early in the twenty-first century, most of the solar/spiritual side of humanity is still struggling to overcome traditionally conditioned limits. In time, Leo will understand that its true heritage is a spiritual one. Then the acting limits of family heritage will be replaced by the unlimited status as offspring of Divinity. Leo is child of the King. Only when we exchange our earthly ruler for a divine one, can Leo come into its true glory. At that time, Leo Saturn will no longer be a fixed boundary, but a corona such as outlines the sun.

### Saturn the Authority Figure

This is the "do as I say, not as I do" placement. Many Leo authority figures are autocratic phonies who have no self-discipline and cannot teach it—except by negative example.

This Saturn is intended to be a benevolent ruler, who rules fairly and with kindness. More often, this person is a spoiled brat, pretending to authority she or he does not have, demanding respect she or he has not earned. Here the hereditary factor looms large. If your authority figure was ruled by a narcissistic parent, s/he is likely to follow in those footsteps, treating you as s/he was treated.

As a consequence, some natives abdicate the throne, refusing to do Saturn duty at all. Their children must then discipline themselves, or not! Children need limits, so these may act out in the attempt to see how far they can go.

Some natives have pretend Authority Figures, some person who has usurped that role in your life. Others make-up limits for themselves, pretending to have an authority figure that does not really exist.

### Saturn the Protector

With Saturn in Leo, the Authority Figure may only pretend to protect you. These great pretenders may seem very protective in public, but in private, you may have to protect yourself from them. Saturn in Leo is often arrogant, demanding a higher level of performance from others than they ever give. They may teach their children public performance designed to enhance the parental reputation.

Leo Saturn is almost always protective of his or her reputation. If you are too protective, it may limit the expression of your highest and best talents, because you are afraid of public opinion. Leo cannot tolerate being criticized or laughed at and will do what is necessary to protect him or herself.

### Personal Space and Boundaries

With this placement, we are dealing with solar boundaries. Consider the Sun. Exactly where are its boundaries? From our perspective it has none. It exists within a corona of light and boundaries of light are highly tenuous. Light expands indefinitely to fill up available space.

Create your own personal space in which your light can shine freely. Do not accept limits that put your talents in shadow.

### Personal Definition

You are intended to define yourself by your Sun—according to its sign plus any planets which closely aspect it. Your Sun is intended to overshadow or outshine your ascendant. An Ascendant is formed from the opinions of the adults in your childhood. Never is it you, but for most people it works reasonably well. Leo Saturn natives will do best by ignoring the opinions of other people. This is one place where you need to exercise the autocratic side of Leo.

We have said that you are authorized to play whatever roles will serve you. That is appropriate, *so long as you remember the actor,* the person who is playing the role. Think of it this way: Did John Wayne ride his horse home at the end of the acting day? Neither should you.

## Responsibility

A common expression of this placement is to use responsibility for children as a limit on self-expression. It is important to notice that having children, taking responsibility for children, is a choice. When you choose children, you choose to be responsible for their care, support, and training for adulthood. That is one of the few near-absolute rules of life. However, children are designed to grow up, to emancipate, to take their freedom and give you yours. The responsibility for children is always temporary, unless you choose otherwise by adopting or fostering a long line of children. To continue to use children as boundaries, you need to get a minimum of one new child every 18 years.

Leo Saturn is sometimes inclined to play with their children, or fight with their children, in lieu of teaching them discipline and boundaries. Again, if you are having trouble here, chose a role model and "play the parent" until you can properly do so.

Even during your parenting years, you should be true to yourself. Express as much of your creativity as you can without harming your children. While you may not be able to quit your job and go to Paris to paint, you can draw pictures for your children and teach them to draw as well. More than that, you can make secret plans for the time when they are emancipated.

## Maturity

Leo Saturn cannot, should not, attempt to conform to rigid conventions of maturity. One may grow up without growing old. That is the brilliance native to Leo. Leo is a star, and stars do not get old for a very long time.

It is important to be mature without being old. This means taking your proper responsibilities—for yourself and your minor children, while remembering that you are designed to express your Self and your talent. You are created to shine your light. If it seems that your corona is moderate in size, remember that the light you spread now, may/will shine down the corridors of time. Light forever travels across the realms of time and space.

Also notice that the sun does not so much act, as activate. Without solar activation, life on earth would end. You are simply a container for light—a lamp, perhaps. Keep your light bright, by doing those things that you love. The joy you feel, the joy you create, is the energy on which the world runs. Never mind maturity. Just be.

## Rights and Authority

Above all, it is your right to shine, to be playful, to enjoy life. Let your limits be simply the limits of joy. You have a right to have fun. You are authorized to live in joy. You are authorized to spread joy, to create joy, to lighten the spirits of self and others.

The master, Jesus ben Joseph, said, "Ye are the light of the world." He meant you. He also said that to enter the kingdom of Heaven you must become as a little child. Leo is the little child[15] of the zodiac. With Saturn in Leo, that is meant to be a description and/or definition of your life.

### Saturn's Law

Leo Saturn's law is the law is the law of creativity. In Judeo-Christian scriptures, we are told that humans were created in the image of Divinity. An image is a mirror. As a child mirrors its physical heritage, so we are also intended to mirror our spiritual heritage–literally the heritage of creativity. Creativity is in our spiritual DNA. As God/dess spoke the world into being, so we are learning to speak our creative word. The more we retain a child-like innocence, the more we stay in touch with our inner child, the more we are able to express our innate creativity.

Today, we call that the creative consciousness. It is another version, perhaps an advancement, on the creative rituals of paganism. The point is, that (co-)creativity is inherent in us all. It is a universal law.

# Saturn in Virgo

Virgo Saturn shows very conscious boundaries. It also reminds us that our limits exist only in consciousness. Virgo is related to consensus reality, so the consensus may have taught you to create boundaries for yourself that have little relevance for your adult life. Above all, you are required to analyze your boundaries.

Saturn in Virgo often shows a command to "remember your limits." He reminds us to color inside the lines. Conditioning is very deep. You have been taught that it is your duty to remember your assigned limits, at all costs. Following the rules has been made a survival issue. If you do not remember to stay within your assigned limits, you may not get your needs met and/or you may not even survive outside the proscribed parameters.

Another implication is that you must earn your way, that you must earn love, care, protection. Obedience is the price of life. There is a feeling of that's just the way it is. Underlying this is the subtle issue of traditional fundamental Churchianity, the doctrine that we must earn our way into Heaven. In it, all of us are guilty and guilt amounts to a debt that must be paid, either out of our struggle, or by some gift of salvation. The popular ideas of Karma carry much the same weight, except that they make you pay on Earth, rather than in Hell.

Clearly, no one can live a perfect life according to these doctrines. Consequently, Virgo Saturn equals limits-of-guilt. Guilt is the most destructive of emotions. It can stop you in your tracks, arresting growth. It can make you sick because if you think that there is something inherently wrong with you, your body may pay the price. Guilt can make you feel unworthy to have more, to be

---

[15]Cancer is the infant. Leo is the school-age child, especially ages 5-10.

more and/or to become more. It is probably the most rigid boundary of all, certainly equal to Leo Saturn. Earth signs may be slightly less rigid than fixed ones, but not by much!

Duty is another big issue for Virgo Saturn. Conditioned duties may be the roadblocks that stop you from growing into your full potential. You feel that you must take care of massive responsibilities before you can be free to follow your own path. This can lead to over-work, even compulsive busyness.

Beneath it all is conditioning about making ourselves useful. Work-a-holics may have to become ill to allow themselves to rest without guilt. This leads to the idea of health as a limit. Poor health may limit what you can do. Equally, good health can be understood as an obligation to take on duties that really belong to others. Notice how certain people (never Saturn in Virgo) use ill health as a control on the lives of others. You may have to learn some tough love, refusing to take care of those who should be "taking up their bed and walking into life." Taking care of the spiritually lazy is <u>not</u> your job!

We all serve a purpose, but that purpose is never to be servant or slave to any other person. Instead serve as a practical model of your spiritual practice and beliefs. Serve your own highest truths.

## Saturn the Authority Figure

Your authority figure may seem to be perfect. It is always wise to look askance at such an evaluation. Even when your Sun, Moon, and Saturn all fall in Virgo, none of the people they represent are perfect examples for your life. Their flaw is in their emotional fastidiousness.

These people give you things instead of time, attention, and respect. They are like professional care-takers who go through all the required motions, but it is only from duty, because it is their job.

By example and/or by word, they teach you that there are rules and boundaries which proscribe your life, and that you live in a black-and-white world, one that just is and not subject to analysis, adaptation or adjustment. These authority figures take their cues from some higher authority, one that does not require you to think about the rules, analyze them for intelligence, or make any choices for yourself.

In reality, the Virgo Authority Figure is a spiritual adolescent, caught between the innocence of childhood and the responsibilities of adulthood. She or he has learned to serve a strict parental Divinity which she or he fears but often does not respect. She or he may discipline/abuse you from a fear of looking like a bad parent. You have to be a perfect child, to make this one look like a perfect parent. Appearance supercedes truth, and serving a purpose supercedes exceeding parental expectations.

This authority figure has a low self-image, a slave or servant mentality. As she or he serves his/her authority, you are expected to serve yours—meaning your Authority Figure. You are also expected to stay within your class. This placement often limits opportunities to develop talents, to educate yourself or in some other way rise above the class into which you were born.

It is imperative to take back your authority over your own life. Be servant to no hu/man. Your life is not intended to be used by others.

**Saturn the Protector**

Virgo Saturn is nothing if not meticulous. He may protect you from an almost endless list of things, especially those things that don't smell right, or things that are useless, or in bad form, or out of order. He may try to protect you from life, holding you in stasis, refusing to let you venture far from your conditioning.

If your Authority Figure held irrational fears, you may be contained by them, in the name of protecting yourself from threats from the unknown. Natives would do well to spend time with their fears and phobias, analyzing them. Are they real? Are they even yours? Could something that made sense long ago have become irrelevant or obsolete? This is an adolescent sign and you are intended to continue your growth into adulthood. This will mean outgrowing some of your inherited tendencies for self-protection in the name of exploring your own potential.

The most important lesson for Virgo Saturn is to practice setting boundaries against irrational fears. It requires you to *choose*, consciously and with intent, to examine your fears, to determine what is real, and to protect yourself from unreal or irrational fearfulness.

**Personal Space and Boundaries**

Your personal space is bounded by Earth limits. You let the fact that you are a physical being define what it is possible to be/do/become. You consider your physicality to be a limit on your beingness. A major realization will be that your body is simply a useful form that spirit takes. Any real limits that your body puts on your life are there to keep you focused on your pre-incarnational purpose and intentions. You actually have the perfect body for accomplishing your spiritual goals.

Your sense of how perfect or imperfect your body—or any body—is, will influence what you think that you can or should do/be/become. There is a sense of needing to have a perfect body or a perfect life. This would be okay if we did not allow others to define perfection for us. In reality, we are, each and all, the perfect us. It is only when we accept another's idea of perfection that we begin to fall short, fall ill, become discouraged, fail.

Claiming your own space and boundaries, working it out for yourself, is a key task with this placement. In essence, it is about moving your boundaries out from your body, to include your whole aura. If you keep your boundaries at the edge of your aura, they will expand naturally as your consciousness grows. As you practice making your own choices, your limits naturally expand to give you more growing room.

Practice is the key to mastery. This placement denotes a commitment to move toward ever greater mastery of living in human form. Your body is not meant to be a limit. It is simply a container, one specially designed for the goals of this incarnation.

## Personal Definition

*Above all, do not define yourself as a servant.* Neither define your life as intended for the achievement of perfection, working out your salvation, or paying some karmic debt. You are dutiful, so what is your duty? Your duty is to be the best you that you can be. Since you were made perfectly for that, begin by designating yourself as the perfect me. Now, what is it that you do best? Practice that, working toward improvement, toward mastery.

It is so important to realize that real boundaries are merely the limits of your particular spiritual level of maturity. Virgo is something of an adolescent, living between a spiritual childhood and spiritual adulthood. Your intent is to grow, and in growing you naturally expand your boundaries. Your true limits are your level of maturation, so remember that, like all teens, you are practicing to become an adult. Give yourself room to make some mistakes. Mistakes are part of learning. If you are making a mistake, you are trying. Spirit will honor your trying. Use your life to take the next step in personal and/or spiritual development.

*Notice:* We said nothing about religion. This placement is seldom comfortable with religion because it denies your right to make your own moral choices. On some level, you know that God/dess is not out there, but resides in you. Look inward for your guidance and you will do well.

## Responsibility

Your true responsibility is to yourself. It is to live a life that makes sense to you, whether or not it does to anyone else. It is not your responsibility to make any other happy.

It is your responsibility to choose what is right and good for you. It is your responsibility to choose how you will use your life, and to use it responsibly. It is your responsibility to emancipate yourself and live as a free individual. It is your responsibility to think for yourself, to do work that you love, to take care of your body and your soul.

You are responsible for your minor children, but only until they are educated. After that, it is your responsibility to let them go, to encourage their independence.

## Maturity

True maturity is leaving home. Like any adolescent, you are meant to outgrow your childhood and its rules. The first Saturn return is particularly important here, for it is the time when we are all authorized to begin making our own rules for living.

By then you should have healthy, realistic limits in place. Most of all, they should be elastic so that there is room for them, for your life, to expand. Keep in mind that you are just in the process of growing into a new phase in spiritual development, a new phase in individuality. Part of maturity is learning to laugh at yourself, to forgive yourself, and keep on keeping on. This is how you eliminate many shoulds and should-nots that have no relevance to your adult life.

### Rights and Authority

Most of all, you have the right to grow in wisdom, and stature, and in favor with God/dess and man. You have the right to make your own choices, especially the choice about whom or what you will serve. You have the right to make mistakes and to try again, as many times as it takes to master each new lesson or task.

Let your limits be flexible, open ended, chosen, changed, and chosen again. Remember that all of us begin life within the limits of a crib, then a house, a yard, a neighborhood, etc.., until by the time we reach our twenties, they may expand to the size of this world.

### Saturn's Law

Saturn's law is the law of choice. It is the law of free will. To us is given the opportunity to use our abilities and potential as we wish. It is the right to be free, to be neither owned nor used by any other. It is the right to serve our own purposes, to set our own boundaries, choose our own limits, to go as far as we choose—and no farther.

Its only condition is that we honor the rights of others in the same way.

## Saturn in Libra

Libra Saturn shows shared boundaries, boundaries that really belong to another/others. Initially, they belong to our first other—M/other. Later they may belong to our significant other, if we use significant-other relationships to separate or free us from our parents.

Because we use other people to define ourselves, to outline our space, to proscribe our potential, we may even use our (adult) children to limit our lives. And if we do, we are holding them down, even as we were held down. We *must* grant them equality as they reach adulthood—including full independence. We must realize that they truly are equal to the task.

With this placement, our primary relationships limit us because we absorb our partner's personal boundaries as our own—often without noticing that we have done so. These limits may be the beliefs, values, or fears, etc. held by another. They will then hinder our individuation and personal growth, unless or until, we see them for what they are and separate us from those with whom we are psychically entangled. We may explain this by saying, "I cannot do this because I am a married wo/man," or "because my spouse needs me," or . . .

Initially, Libra Saturn usually indicates that we feel less than whole in ourselves. We may not feel equal to the task or equal to others. As a result, we may feel equally limited by the lack of a partner, feeling that we cannot do certain things as a single adult. This placement makes it critical to review all our scripts that say, "I cannot do this because _____." See box.

In the more abstract sense, planets in Libra are married to their polar opposite. Here, we see Saturn married to the Moon. Lunar needs are thus equal to, and united with, Saturn's limits. In practice, this means that your idea of what you need, becomes a boundary on what you can have.

In some way (consciously or unconsciously) you have accepted the idea that you cannot have more than you need.

However, anything linked to this pair is also linked to growth/Moon and maturation/Saturn. Recognizing growing needs will quite naturally push your boundaries outward. If you can think of Saturn as functioning like your skin, you will be on your way to increasing your personal space and potential.

## Notepad and Pencil

For at least a week, carry a small notepad and pen or pencil. Every time you hear yourself think or say, "I cannot do this because _____" write it down. After you have a list, take some quiet time and carefully review each item.

Is it really true that you cannot do this?

Is it even true that your partner/parent could not do it? If so, how have times or the situation changed?

What do you need to do to free yourself of this limit? Is there a way to accomplish this by myself?

What will happen if I make God/dess my partner?

Repeat the exercise from time to time. We recommend it at the beginning of each calendar or personal year.

Attached to this is another necessity, if you are to pursue greater expression of your core being. With Libra limits, it is critical that you formulate your Mars-Desire thoughts in a specific way. See box.

Claim what you want as the spiritual need that it is, and you get past your own inhibiting conditioning.

Mars = Wants = Desires

De-Sire means "of the Father." Your desires are the needs of your spirit. They are what The Father wants for you, and what you are destined to have. When we refuse to reach for them, we deny our own spiritual heritage and purpose.

Libra's evolutionary level comes into play here. The first six signs of the zodiac represent separation-from-the wholeness. Aries begins the journey to consciousness of our physicality, until, in Virgo, we are physically perfect, whole, and complete–even though religion may say otherwise! With that established, we are ready to begin the return to wholeness. Libra is the first phase of the journey, where we begin to reunite body and spirit. At first, we may think this a choice to be made, but it is not. It is really about the marriage of body and spirit, and about realizing their equality. It is the beginning of knowing that we are half-animate, half-divine and that one side is not better than the other. These are the two halves that make a whole.

As the various planets and points of our charts pass through Libra, each begins this return- to-wholeness, by trying to create a balance between their physical and spiritual meanings. In practice, this has the effect of uniting each planet with its polar opposite[16], each point (as Ascendant-Descendant) with its polarity. The Libra placement of Saturn makes it equal with your Moon. It also forges a partnership, as described above.

16 See Appendix II

## Saturn the Authority Figure

The downside of Libra is judgment. Your authority figure is judgmental. She or he compares you to another—usually in a negative way that makes you feel inadequate. This judgment stands between you and your ability to push your boundaries, leaving you uncertain of your right and/or ability to do so. The first thing you must realize is that your authority figure holds authority only by size. She or he is not wiser nor more mature than you. In reincarnational terms, she or he is not even more experienced than you. As you mature, it may be necessary to stop habitually comparing yourself to others in a negative way.

Your authority figure is really your spiritual equal–or, we may say that you are theirs. By this we mean that you are born their spiritual equal. If you grow at all, you will become their superior . . . and you will grow. By word or deed these authority figures may try to hold you down to their level. These are the people who say or imply, "All humans are created equal; if a head sticks up above the crowd, cut it off!"

They may also say, "Fit in. Don't be different. Don't stand out." In childhood, this message came from parents/mother and other authority figures, either verbally or subliminally. As an adult, you are likely to hear it coming from your spouse, your boss, or the cop on the beat! Consequently, when you begin to push your limits, you may find the world full of adversaries. There are always people who want to keep us in our place, harnessed to the needs of others. Claim the Aries polarity and fight for your right to a fair share of life's goodness.

The Libra Authority figure is still uncertain of his/her authority. Like one just beyond adolescence, they are trying out skills learned in their (evolutionary) youth. Easily threatened, and somewhat paranoid, they often waver between too much discipline and too little. They may give you too much responsibility in some areas and not enough in others. This can cause your maturation to proceed by fits and starts. It will be difficult to determine what is and what is not your responsibility as you move into adulthood. Chances are you are too responsible in some areas and not responsible enough in others. It is common, with this placement, to have difficulty taking enough responsibility for yourself, because you are carrying too many others on your back. Learn to create a balance, with the emphasis on fair treatment for yourself.

## Saturn the Protector

Our authority figure is responsible for protecting us. When placed in Libra, that protection may be uneven and quite erratic, because s/he cannot protect you from his or her own fears. Most often the two of you stand together for protection from the outside world.

Sometimes a parent teaches you his or her own methods of protection instead. These may consist of hiding from or, distracting potential attackers. Alternatives are the use of mind-altering substances to numb the fears. Other times, you and s/he partner to protect others, as younger siblings.

Your most important lesson will be learning to trust your inner partner to protect you. That

Saturn in the Signs

partner has unlimited resources to do so. You may utilize this protection through use of boundary-setting. See box, Setting Boundaries.

## Personal Space and Boundaries

Your personal space is bounded by mental and/or relational (air) limits. This means other people, and more specifically the society into which you were born set the limit on what you can do/be/become, on where and how far you can go in life. Social boundaries may continue to limit you until you realize that it takes individual action to change them.

So long as others define your space, it is never stable and you will have no defensible boundaries.

## Setting Boundaries

Visualize or affirm a circle drawn around yourself. Make it small at first if you need to, as you must be able to believe it exists. Inside that circle is your space and you make the rules. Choose what energies and experiences you will allow inside the circle and what you want kept out. Example: Only honest and trustworthy people can enter. This means that dishonest, untrustworthy people must change or leave. Always set the rules based on behavior, not individual people.

The size of, and rules for, your circle can change at will, according to need and your comfort zone. You will find it much easier to keep unwanted experience out of your life than to learn how to deal with it once it gets in.

Demand fair and equitable treatment. Declare your authority over your own life. Take back your right to live, move and breathe.

Move your focus to the center of your space and let your boundaries move outward like rings from a pebble dropped into a pond. Even better, take the horizon as a boundary. It always forms a circle with you at the center. When you move toward it, it moves ahead of you. Learning to stay centered in your own space may be the most important personal task of your life.

## Personal Definition

Defining yourself as Other will limit your life. Even Equal can be limiting. Instead, move to the other side and use words like Mediator, Medium and Peacemaker. These will allow you much more room to move. They move you from opposite some significant other to a middle ground, where you can balance between responsibilities to yourself and responsibilities to others. Here you take your share of responsibility, without taking on too much or too little. Here you are equal to almost any task.

## Responsibility

Your most important responsibility is to yourself. If you do not take care of, provide for and protect yourself, you will have nothing to share with the world, nothing to give to others. This placement most often fails by taking on responsibility for others who are really equals–and equal to the task. So long as you are not clear about your responsibilities to and for yourself, you will attract moochers/takers who are only too willing to let you take on their responsibilities. You will find your home filled with adults unwilling to behave like adults. You will find the workplace filled with people who are all too willing to let you do more than your share of the work.

Libra Saturn insists that you weigh the alternatives, that you keep life in balance. If you do not claim your right to equal treatment, you will not get it. The secret to this comes from a fundamentalist saying, "God and I make a majority." With God/dess as my defining partner, there is nothing I cannot do, be or become. I am equal to whatever comes up. Let these words be an affirmation of your right to be all that you were meant to be, to have all that is rightfully yours, and to keep pushing your limits outward.

## Maturity

True maturity brings independence and the capacity to make your own rules, define your own limits, and to change them as needed. Maturity is an individual process. In spite of Libra, <u>we do not mature in tandem or in harness.</u> We mature when we stop comparing ourselves to others. The only rational comparison to make is to our own past, as we learn to challenge the old boundaries, forever pushing our own limits, while remaining centered in our own space.

Individuation is a necessary part of maturation. Individuation requires certain space boundaries to protect our person. We need to be clear about how close we want others, and what we will allow them to do to us. Shared boundaries are no protection, so let us move Libra into a new dimension. Take note that although your freedom ends where the other person's begins, their freedom also ends where yours begins. Remember that Libra is not merely Partner. It is also Adversary. Advocate for your own life, your own space, first. Once that is established, you can safely share your life with others. This is full maturity.

## Authority and Rights

You have the authority and the right to call upon your higher power. You do not need a mediator or priest/tess to stand between you and your Deity. You have the right to be treated equally, to have your own inviolable space. Sharing does not mean that *you give and everyone else takes.* Only equals can truly share. Only equals are appropriate partners. You have a right to an equal share of all things in life, whether it be property, success, or joy. Insist on equal rights.

## Saturn's Law

Saturn's Law is the Law of Balance. It refers to a balance of physical and spiritual energies, needs, and desires. Ultimately it reminds us that we are both physical and spiritual beings and that physicality is an equal partner with spirituality. We are half physical, half divine, the perfect blend of physical and spiritual DNA.

# Saturn in Scorpio

Saturn in Scorpio can only limit us according to our definition and evaluation of personal power. Power is neutral. Only its use can be good or evil. The power to do, is simply the ability to do. It is competency. This placement is intended to confer the right to use power based on the evolutionary maturity that we have achieved.

With this placement, only conditioning based on negative evaluations of personal power and/or our right to use it can hinder us. Still, these are common. When we are born more powerful, more competent than certain adults in our childhood, they may feel threatened by our power. They may then use their superior size to control us, making us feel powerless, even as they teach us to define power as control. Out of this may come a fear or hatred of authority that will invest our power in defenses. This will, in turn, deplete our creative energy.

Parents sometimes harness their children's power for their own uses. This is done by teaching us that love requires the competent to take care of the incompetent. The enabling of incompetency is not love and the teaching that love means loss of power is a lie. Sometimes it takes years to understand that we have been coerced into limiting ourselves to inferior levels of performance. Perhaps the worst of all parental errors is teaching children that loving others means investing our highest and best in supporting the lack of growth in others. Teaching others or leading them is one thing. Doing for them, what they should be doing for themselves is quite another.

In older generations, Scorpio Saturn usually meant *fused* limits. This means that you absorbed your mother's boundaries, through the mother-child bond. It suggests that a significant part of her emotional state was related to being under the control of another—usually her mother.

This may go generations deep. During your developmental years, your Mother was still struggling against her mother's control. Her emotional turmoil was overwhelming and got absorbed by (you) the infant she carried "in her body and in her arms." Her feeling of being controlled, or fighting for control, saturated your developing response system and was accepted as your own. You may feel about your mother as she felt about hers—with or without cause.

Scorpio is also the sign of transformation–specifically the transformation from child to adult. The taboos of childhood (such as using your power) become major assets when you claim your adulthood, your independence, your right to act in your own best interests. In the final analysis, Saturn in Scorpio confers the right to do anything that you have the power to do. This is personal power, and it is critical that you use it first for yourself, including your minor offspring. Only as there is energy left over, is it acceptable to use it for others. Even then, it is only truly moral to help those who are willing to help themselves, those who are struggling to grow into their own potential potency/power.

## Saturn the Authority Figure

This can be the best or the worst of Authority Figures. Frequently this Authority Figure is abusive. They use their power to abuse those smaller or weaker than themselves, such as their children.

With Saturn in Scorpio you may need protection from your Authority Figure. Rarely do you get any protection from him or her. Instead, you get blame. Blame is the only acknowledgment of a child's power that most adults give. They blame the child for their own lack of discipline and/or self-control.

This Authority Figure is also the Power Figure–and usually feminine. She is the clear head of household, the person who makes and enforces the rules. She also controls the purse strings and who gets what. Usually, s/he is a competent manager, but she uses her competence to manage the people in her life in ways that keep them under her control.

At its apparent-best, the particular combination of authority and power represented here, manifests as an Authority Figure who believes that they know what is best for others and coerces them accordingly. Scorpio is a powerfully magnetic sign, and when prominent in a chart, one can have almost hypnotic influence on others. This can be absorbed as a moral imperative for you, so that it continues to control your life. To the infant and toddler, the Authority Figure is God/dess. Consequently, it may be years before either of you notice that this is another form of control.

**Saturn the Protector**

You really have no protector because the person you most need protection from is your Authority Figure. And if truth be told, your innate power is sufficient that you could defend yourself if you were willing to do so. But, having accepted superior size as a right to control, you accept coercion and/or physical abuse in the name of love.

With this placement we learn to control our impulse for self protection and preservation to protect our abusers. This may be from an innate understanding that, as children, we need adults to provide the necessities for our growing bodies. It may also be from a reluctance to take responsibility for disciplining those to whom tradition has given authority over us. Either way, the key to taking back your power later in life will be to understand that, had you not inhibited your natural instincts for self-preservation, your abusers might have paid dearly for their behavior. Instead, you allowed their abuse on the grounds that you could take it, that you could survive it. You may even have made yourself a target to protect others using the same reasoning. For full control of your own power, you must stop volunteering as a target for the ill will of others, even if it means severing family connections or friendships.

**Personal Space and Boundaries**

While our boundaries remain entangled with our mother's, we feel as limited or unlimited as she does. Whatever she believes that she can or cannot do/be/become is what we believe that we can or cannot do/be/become.

Still, we have the power to disentangle our limits from hers, by the simple act of taking back our power. This means breaking her control on our lives. It also means declaring our independence from her and our right to live by our own authority. When we do not, we may simply transfer control of our lives from our parental authority to spousal management.

## Personal Definition

A great deal of what happens depends on your personal definition. If you accept a title of the one to blame, you will continue to allow others to control your life on the grounds that you have no right to live for yourself. If you name yourself the one in control, you may violate the rights of others. The correct definition of Self is a statement, "I am in control of my life and my destiny. I take responsibility for myself and use my personal power responsibly."

With this placement, you can become an authority in your own right. It is the power to be self-actualized, and to be invested with (divine) power. That power comes from your higher self—or your God/dess. Literally Saturn in Scorpio refers to an evolutionary level that confers the right to use/channel Divine Power for creation and transformation in our lives. If you allow that power to define you, nothing will be impossible to you.

## Responsibility

Our first responsibility is self-control. This means taking control of our own lives, without attempting to control others. Often this requires detachment from assumed obligations that were never ours to take on. It means allowing others the responsibility for themselves and the right to face the consequences of their own actions.

This placement is about using power responsibly and that means neither controlling others, nor allowing them to control us. Competency is not a lien on our lives. The only absolute responsibility that we have is to our minor children. To allow parents, adult siblings or offspring to live off our energy/money is not a loving act. It may even be a form of controlling others and it certainly limits your own life and freedom.

## Maturity

Your personal power is a mark of spiritual maturity. Never should personal power be a limit on our lives. Reclaiming your power is your first maturation priority. The second is the willingness to use the power given you for your own highest good, and the recognition that this will, automatically, be the best for others.

In later years, this placement can bring a position of influence when power is managed well. Full maturity recognizes the purpose of personal power as creativity, applied to creating a life worthy of emulation. Here, the word spoken with authority, (without doubt) is highly creative.

Maturity means learning to love your power, to value its capacity to create the good things in life. This kind of power is worthy of love. The final Scorpio fusion is of Love and Power. It is knowing that positive regard is the most valuable power on Earth, a force that can create anything, even life itself.

## Authority and Rights

As we have said, Saturn in Scorpio is, quite literally, the right to have and use personal power. You are an authorized agent of Deity. It is neither authority nor power over others. It is the right and the power to become co-creators with our God/dess. It is a priestly placement.

It is the point in personal evolution where we are invested with authority, given the right to use power-from-above to create good in human lives. It grants the ability to concentrate attention for creation. Positive attention creates good. Negative attention creates not-good. You have been given the authority and the power to bless and to curse. Use it wisely. Use it well.

## Saturn's Law

This is the Law of Power, the power that comes from merging spirit and form. Divine intelligence and creative power flow through humanity as awareness and/or attention. This energy is the very source and sustenance of human life. At this level, we are limited only by the amount

of power we allow to flow through our lives. When we consciously use focused attention, physical strength is replaced by the magical and/or miraculous. Trading *will power* for *willingness power*, we become a channel for the continuing flow of life and more abundant life.[17]

The only limit there can be is the one we set ourselves.

# Saturn in Sagittarius

This Saturn is ruled by Jupiter, who forever follows Saturn, pushing him outward. All limits are intended to be temporary and movable. When Saturn is in Sagittarius, an otherwise Jolly Jupiter may get quite insistent. He will expand your awareness, even if he must first magnify your boundaries to the point of smothering you. Consequently, Saturn often seems very large indeed.

However, Jupiter is the greatest salesman of the solar system, and he will not take "no" for an answer, even from Saturn. He intends that your only boundary be the moving horizon.

You will outgrow your conditioned limits, replacing many of the rules-to-live-by that were taught you in childhood, as you design a very personal morality.

Saturn in Sagittarius refers to limits of belief, boundaries set by a belief system that we

have accepted as truth. Often he wears the robes of a priest or minister insisting that you accept some dogma without question. Intended to mean traveling boundaries or expanding boundaries, this placement will expand your limits by whatever means are necessary, including a temporary loss of faith.

At its best, this placement refers to an innate understanding of the purpose and use of limits. When you question the limits of your inherited belief system, you will find a deeper truth. You may come to understand that the true purpose of limits is focus.

---

[17]Quote from Jesus ben Joseph—Jn. 10:10

The key to seeing is not-seeing the background clutter. The key to hearing is not-hearing the background static. A proper use of Saturn is the fine-tuning of perceptions. Saturn is also useful to outline or define that which you wish to create. Let Saturn sketch or describe what you intend to envision/create.

Most importantly, let Saturn redefine the words you use, beginning with limits and boundaries. Rename them temporary constructs, used for a specific purpose and then discarded, and you will have mastered Saturn.

With Saturn in Sagittarius, you have mastered using boundaries in this way during past lives. You understand their purpose and use. You have only to suspend whatever conditioned beliefs stand between you and remembering this.

Many people begin that process with a simple polarity reversal. Christians convert to Buddhism or Paganism. Buddhists or Pagans may convert to Christianity. Another common change is to change forms of Christianity, as from Catholicism to fundamentalism, or from traditional to metaphysical Christianity. This solves very little, but out of it may come a very personal kind of faith which usually synthesizes several belief systems.

---

## Changing Truth

Like everything else, truth changes over time.

It was once true that man could not fly. Today it is true that we can fly, even to the Moon, if we use the proper vehicle.

Even now, a few people do astral travel and fly without machines.

Teleportation comes next. One day it will be true that all of us can fly in this way. Then the new truth will be that everyone can fly!

---

**Saturn the Authority Figure**

This Authority Figure is often The Church. Here church dogma has usurped parental authority and/or become an excuse for parental abuse. Saturn becomes a denial of the right to question some authority by divine right, whether administered by pope, pastor, priest or parent. It is belief masquerading as truth. And so long as you believe it, it will be your truth.

A common adage is, "I will believe it when I see it." At this evolutionary level that statement is transformed to "I will see it when I believe it." Consequently, the only limit on what you can do is what you believe that you cannot or should not do.

The great wonder of this is that when you change your beliefs, you change your limits. Accept the possibility that you have more potential than you thought and those limits begin to move outward. Forgive yourself for accepting limits that are obsolete or irrational. Set yourself free to discover your own reality, your own truth. This will make you your own Authority Figure–as you were intended to be.

## Saturn the Protector

The family Authority Figure may be a liar, from whom you need protection and/or she or he may consistently break promises. S/he may teach you to lie because truth hurts.[18] This protector often abandons his or her responsibility to protect, parenting by the old proverb, "Spare the rod and spoil the child." It becomes an excuse for child abuse by parents and sometimes by religious leaders.

Consequently you must protect yourself, in whatever way that you can. These protections may then limit you later in life. Above all else, you need to understand your responses. Once you are aware of outworn habits of self-protection, you can begin to heal the wounds to your soul. In time, the protections learned in childhood will no longer limit you.

Notice that you have survived and retained a reasonable degree of sanity in circumstances where others have not. Let this tell you that you are self and/or divinely protected, and that you entered this environment knowing that.

Above all, know this: *If your life, or your sanity are in danger, the only sensible thing to do is to run!*

## Personal Space and Boundaries

In one way or another, you will need plenty of space. Let no other tell you how much space you need in your inter-personal relationships. Abandon those who insist on invading your space. You are not designed for emotional closeness to more than a few people. At the same time, you do very well with easy friendships that do not violate your personal boundaries.

Having been abandoned by your protector, you may appear to distrust closeness.

Allowing close relationship seems to bring up abandonment issues, but the truth is that you know, instinctively, whom you should let touch your aura and whom you should avoid.

Life has taught you that wisdom is the better part of valor, and that putting space between you and many another is the simplest way of protecting both body and soul. Consequently, you have learned to be far more emotionally independent than most. Although you like and enjoy people, you can survive on your own and do not need others in the way that most people do.

## Personal Definition

Initially, you may define yourself as a believer—Christian, Pagan, etc. As time passes, you may overturn your original belief system, replacing it with an opposite–as Christian turning Pagan or Buddhist—or vice versa. Eventually, you will need to rename yourself a truth-seeker. This will allow your concept of truth to expand exponentially, through a synthesis of several or many belief systems.

---

[18]This is particularly interesting in Indigos, who will not lie. They will tell the truth, and bluntly. They are not afraid of what even much bigger people can do to them.

In the end, it is not so important what belief system you begin with, as it is that you make it a foundation on which to build, or a home base from which to explore. Doing this, neither the original belief system, nor its replacement will define or limit you. In some way, you are a designated disseminator of information who crosses the boundaries of belief systems to discover and teach eternal truths.

## Responsibility

The primary responsibility for Sagittarius Saturn is to grow in consciousness, to become aware of greater personal potential, wider applications of principle, and to seek his or her own truth. For us, truth will ever be exactly what we believe it to be. If our belief is small and limiting, our lives will be confined within those limits.

Consequently, our first responsibility is to question our beliefs, to weed out any that seem unreasonable, and to expand our personal horizons. In the final analysis, our primary responsibility is to live our highest truth.

## Maturity

Maturation is clearly defined as wisdom. Wisdom comes with expanding horizons. It is about discovering more of what we are, and what we can become. It is the search for ever higher truths. It is walking toward the horizon, watching it move ahead of us, and realizing that our willingness to travel, in time, space, or consciousness is the only measure or limit on our potential for wisdom.

Finally, it is the discovery that we really have no limits except those we acquire by relinquishing control of our thinking to others. Only as our belief-systems are open ended, do we mature as we were designed to do.

## Rights and Authority

It is your right to be respected for your wisdom. You have the right, even the mandate, to run away when your life or sanity are threatened. Wisdom is the better part of valor. You have the right to choose your own beliefs, to discover your own truths.

You have the right to travel, in space, time and/or consciousness. You are authorized to teach, to broadcast and/or publish the truths you have discovered in your journeys. You have the right to blaze new trails in space and/or in consciousness. You are designed for intellectual leadership.

## Saturn's Law

The Law of Truth states that truth ever expands as we question the limits of our beliefs. It may also be called the Law of Growth, especially growth-in-consciousness. The only absolute truths are the basic principles of life, and these are few. Even these may be questioned or expanded in time. Sagittarius always contains some sense of tomorrow, and the future.

Each principle is the core or nucleus of a concept. As consciousness expands, so do our concepts. We learn newer and larger applications of the basic truths. In this way we grow to ever greater levels of (self) awareness. This is the law that sets us free–free to be, to grow, to become ever more. It is the capacity to understand more, to know more, to reach for the stars.

# Saturn in Capricorn

As any planet crosses Capricorn, it has reached an evolutionary limit. It has become the most and best that it can be \*while remaining within the current definition of human capacity*. To move Capricorn boundaries, we must become more than (hu)man. We must move into the potentiality of our spiritual selves.

This is the placement intended to begin the redefinition of the term <u>human</u>, expanding it exponentially, to include more of the intuitive/instinctive, the visionary, and (magical) creativity. Being born at such a time, we have incarnated to take part in the movement toward greater self awareness in the general population. It is about increasing the percentage of the human brain in use, and/or activating previously dormant areas of DNA.

Saturn in Capricorn can be heavy indeed, and may look like a brick wall. Some natives are subject to depression, just because it feels like they have no place to go, no room to grow.

Life begins in an environment where discipline is traditional and looms large. Saturn may seem a stern and harsh taskmaster. When he does, it is because humanity so often resists change, because it has rejected the idea of human evolution, and/or because it has accepted a god of judgment and punishment. If you try to stay within the limits of human definition, Saturn in Capricorn can feel like you are living in a personal hell. When it hurts you enough, when it almost strangles you,

then you will break out of physical, Earth traditions and reach for a greater sense of self.

Realizing the incompleteness and obsolescence of the existing definition of the word human, you gain the freedom to expand it. With this placement we begin life no more limited that the top 10 per cent (or less) of the population, so any attempt to break out of conditioned restrictions, to overcome them or push them outward will take us beyond the limits experienced

by our parents, grandparents, or even older siblings. People with Saturn in Capricorn are designed to overcome the restrictions of the past through the simple act of setting new and higher goals of achievement for the Self. The authority is given, but it must be accepted. When it is not, your limits get tighter and tighter, and life shrinks accordingly.

### Saturn the Authority Figure

The Capricorn Authority figure is mature and often an older person. With this placement it is common to have parents who are contemporary with the grandparents of your peers—physically and/or psychologically. They will be old fashioned in their ideas of what is possible. They may be harsh disciplinarians while you are young but too tired to do much parenting as you near adolescence.

By the time you are in your teen years, you may be the only authority figure that you have. You must then make your own rules, defining right and wrong for yourself, and deciding for yourself what is or is not possible. You are authorized to do that.

## Saturn the Protector

The only real protection that you have is your own maturity. You are responsible for your own guidance and protection. Here, much depends on other chart factors, and whether you are naturally inclined toward maturity and responsibility. If not, you may overreach yourself, and have to deal with consequences. Probably you will learn self-discipline as you go, and become more self-protective. At best, you will achieve a sense of authority and become a good manager of your own life.

## Personal Space and Boundaries

In a very real sense, the past initially defines your personal space, and its limits. All too often, natives never get past what seems to be a barrier between them and the future. Saturn is at its strongest and most traditional in Capricorn. Only as the individual claims the authority to do so, can s/he break out of the social box assigned by family and birth environment. Until then Saturn continues to contain you within the laws and rules of the past. In the past, the belief that physical expression forever separated us from Divine Spirit held us imprisoned, so that only death could set us free.

The evolved Capricorn Saturn understands that the boundary between spirit and form is an artificial one. Spirit is eternal. It takes form for a specific purpose. Understanding that, the veil thins and we begin to see through the boundary of physicality. The redefinition that every Capricorn Saturn is intended to make is that form is merely an expression or facet of Spirit. With that knowledge we retrieve the potential to become more than (merely) human. With it, we may begin to claim our spiritual genetics, our Divine DNA.

## Personal Definition

Here the self-definition as only human <u>must</u> expand. To achieve the success that Capricorn Saturn promises, we must redefine ourselves as the Elder Brothers and Sisters of humanity. We have always seemed old for our age. That is because, in evolutionary terms, we are older than most of our apparent contemporaries. Being more mature from birth, we are intended to lead others into more successful ways of living. The most successful way of all, applies the laws of Spirit to the tasks of physicality. Saturn in Capricorn is designed to overcome our old definition, and to move us into the first stages of widening perceptual bands, increased intuitive and/or creative abilities. At its best, this placement defines us as one who manages life in such a way as to prove the worth of going beyond the limits of the past, to reach for future possibilities.

## Responsibilities

When Saturn is working properly, with every responsibility comes some degree of authority. All too often, young Capricorn natives are handed adult responsibility without the necessary authority to go with it. Often an eldest child, natives may be expected to keep younger siblings safe, without having the authority to teach them discipline. Expected to be assistant parents, they may struggle mightily to manage the behavior of siblings without having the right to correct them.

Whatever form responsibilities take, natives are responsible for their own survival, almost from birth. No one protects them. No one guides them. They are expected to know what to do in all circumstances. This forces us to reach deep into our inner resources, and there we find that we do have our own sense of what is right and wrong for us to do.

As adults, most natives have a natural aura of authority, that attracts respect and honor. Others look up to us as role models and come to us with their problems and questions. It is our responsibility to claim that authority.

## Maturity

Most natives are mature beyond their years from birth. They will seem older than their years at the beginning of life. However, as they mature, they begin to expand their personal boundaries, to reclaim their authority and rights. At this point, they may seem to reverse the aging process for several years. In their latter years they may look, and usually think quite young relative to their chronological age.

## Authority and Rights

You have the right to manage your own life as you see fit. You are authorized to delegate responsibility, and to hold positions of authority. You also have the right to say "no" to those who would dump their responsibilities on you.

You have the right to be treated with honor, to be respected by your peers. Most of all, you have the right to expand the human definition into which you were born, to develop new human potential, to push human limits to a new level.

## Saturn's Law

This is the law of limits. It states that all boundaries are temporary and related to levels of maturity. Each is intended to protect a specific period of human growth and development. No limit is ever intended to inhibit personal and spiritual growth or human evolution.

When we reach Capricorn, our human limits become our own responsibility. At this time, issues of responsibility, discipline and protection are given into our hands. It becomes our right and our responsibility to set our own limits and to move them as we will.

# Saturn in Aquarius

Saturn enters a new phase in Aquarius, one in which many previously-held limits are broken. Here begins a new definition of humanity that exceeds the norm previously held in the general consciousness. From birth, these children expect to transcend social limits, to break them down, or fly over them. They intend to achieve more than could have been expected at the time of their birth.

Saturn in Aquarius can be defined as broken boundaries, limits or laws. Natives are usually law abiding, but they break the laws of probability and sometimes the laws of physics. A few even seem to break the law of gravity!

Aquarius Saturn is on the move, reaching for the future, for the stars, for a place in the history of the Universe. His/hers is an impersonal calling, one that reaches beyond probability into possibility. The statement, "The sky is the limit," belongs to this placement. Natives naturally take it for granted that they can do anything that anyone else can do, and more. They know and do not question how they know. Naturally inspired in their drive toward the realization of hopes and wishes, it does not occur to them to think that they are limited in their capacity to achieve.

At the same time, natives are humble and, if anything limits them, it is their sense that they are ordinary, not special, not unique. They usually take their uniqueness and gift for inspiration and invention for granted. Overlooking their own genius, they may also be overlooked by others, so they often go without praise, rewards, raises and promotions due them.

Part of the movement toward universal consciousness, this is a relatively small, and very unique group, existing at any given time. These are the originals who are role models for the future of humanity. Existing outside ordinary expectations, many go unseen and unsung for years. Seldom highly visible, their natural or conditioned humility causes them to be ignored and overlooked.

Still, part of the reason for this is that they exceed the expectations of society. People do not see what they believe is impossible. Aquarius Saturn routinely does the impossible. Consequently, their great deeds may seem transparent and largely invisible.

## Saturn the Authority Figure

Your Authority Figure probably took his or her own intelligence, and yours, for granted. This person may seem detached, with wandering thoughts elsewhere, as s/he ignores your apparent need for limits. In reality, he or she is not ignoring it, but rather recognizing your ability to choose your own limits and rules. She or he is allowing you your own authority. There is a transparency here, that allows and expects you to know how far you can go, how great you can be.

Your Authority Figure is not a disciplinarian, but a role model. She teaches by example, and her most important teaching is that there are no limits to what you can do, or whom you can be. She or he models a kind of Universal Citizenship that does not discriminate or judge others. Consequently, you naturally follow his or her lead. In later years, your Authority Figure will be your (best) friend.

## Saturn the Protector

Your Authority Figure may not have given you the protection that you wanted or thought you needed. She or he seemed not to be paying attention, and you may resent that in early adulthood. You will probably forgive this in time, realizing that you chose the parents that you needed and wanted. More than that, although s/he did not protect your body, she or he did nurture and protect your soul, allowing you the freedom to expand your horizons exponentially.

Above all, she or he did not try to confine you to the rules of the past, but left you free to create and re create your own future. She or he trusted you to know what you were doing, and she or he was right!

## Personal Space and Boundaries

This Saturn needs plenty of room to move ahead in life. Your sense of space is closely related to the concept of time, and your movement occurs more in time than space. Only ignoring your own hopes and dreams can limit the room for accomplishment and acquisition. You know how to move beyond the beliefs and expectations of parents and teachers.

Attempts by others to limit your potential get ignored, as you fade out the limits of the past. You focus intently on creation of the future. To you, the past is only a foundation to build upon.

## Personal Definition

With Saturn in Aquarius, your personal definition should be an impersonal one. You are not here for a few individuals, but to take on an impersonal and universal role. You are designed to leave your mark on history. Even though you are not inclined to boast, you need to recognize and own your genius for creating and fulfilling the outlines that become future reality. Name yourself Friend to Humanity, non-judgmental, and future-oriented. Doing this, will set you free to accomplish a great deal. In that accomplishment, you raise the bar for humanity, expanding possibilities exponentially.

## Responsibility

It is your responsibility to go beyond expectations at the time of your birth, to be more, to do more, to become more. It is the responsibility of the advanced and evolved soul who is an elder brother/sister to the general population. It is not your responsibility to do for them, but to be the living example of how to do for themselves. Your life becomes the outline for future generations.

## Maturity

Born mature, you live out the potential of the ONE Spirit, living as one human. In you, the union of spirit and form is made manifest. As the years advance, you do not so much grow in consciousness, as you become increasingly visible. As you learn to see how truly unique you are, will you realize the uniqueness of your purpose. Then and only then will you begin to get the recognition that you deserve.[19]

When you learn to fully value your uniqueness, to realize that you are spiritually gifted, and that you have incarnated, to fulfill dharma, not karma, your life begins to manifest its potential in visible ways. This, above all, is what you came for. You are intended to show the way, but first you must become visible. You must learn to turn up your light, and let it shine brightly. For you, maturity consists of just that. First see yourself, so that others may see you. After that they will they follow.

## Authority and Rights

You have a right to shine, to be unique, to go as far as your hopes and wishes can take you. You have a right to make all your dreams come true, to create your future in unique and special ways. You have a right (and a responsibility) to be different from what is generally expected—of your gender, your family, your generation.

You have a right to ignore many social rules, to transcend accepted human limits, to be more and do more that most of the people around you. You are authorized to live out the future potential of humanity, to demonstrate the versatility available to us all as offspring of Divinity.

## Saturn's Law

This is the law of evolution, of change, of advanced knowledge. It is the outline of the future. It is the potential for development of greater portions of the brain and the catalyst for turning on previously unused DNA. And in the final analysis it is the law which makes life ongoing. It states that, so long as we continue to grow and evolve, we carry the torch of eternal life.

# Saturn in Pisces

Anything in Pisces comes just before the joining of the circle of life, where past and future meet. Pisces is the sign of wholeness, where individuality is lost in unity. Pisces Saturn is both the best and the worst of placements. It neither limits nor seems to protect.

Sometimes this placement suggests the beginning of a new cycle of incarnation, as we emerge from an unlimited past, relative to one level, into the beginning of a new level, with new and unknown rules, limits or duration. Still, unaware of the rules for the new level, natives often do the impossible.

This Saturn is Master of Boundaries. Natives have mastered the use of boundaries in earlier incarnations. They are authorized to use them as they will. There are no limits on what they are allowed to do, and few, if any, on their ability-to-do. If they have boundaries at all, those boundaries are unconscious, therefore nearly invisible. The only limitations they can have are the limits on their faith and trust in themselves, in the rationality of the Universe, and/or in their God/dess.

Even conditioned boundaries are few, tenuous, and nearly transparent. Natives automatically

---

[19]Very often not until your early forties or later.

reach through, walk through, and live beyond, the generally accepted limits of their time. They take themselves for granted, and it may be a long time before it occurs to them that they have no pre-established limits, or that they could set their own limits for protection. Most walk unprotected through life and survive against all odds. Even the law of averages does not seem to apply to them.

Another way to interpret Pisces Saturn is forgotten boundaries. Most seem to have forgotten that there have ever been limits to what they can be or do. They also forget that they can set boundaries around their personal space for protection. Consequently, others continually invade their space with thoughts, emotions and sometimes physical violation or abuse.

On the positive side, once they notice the need, natives easily create boundaries through the use of word and thought, to protect themselves from psychic contamination, physical threat, and/ or energy theft. Contamination comes from the atmosphere around them, because they are born without space boundaries. So, also do physical attacks and violations, which result from having others enter their aura/space with or without intent. Some apparent attacks are the result of inadvertent trespass on their physical space.

Wherever one can live without boundaries, there <u>must be</u> a powerful flow of energy. Only boundaries or pressure can contain and direct any flow, and life is a flow. Certain psychic vampires regard an unbounded flow of life as free food, and they will come running from

everywhere. At some point, natives <u>must</u> learn to set some defensive boundaries, because although permanent damage cannot be inflicted, this kind of interference will damage the quality of life and/or the rate of progress.

**Saturn the Authority Figure**

In reality, these natives have no higher human authority. However, their parents, teachers and certain others seldom accept that. They will attempt to discipline or contain the young Piscean Saturn. A common method of containing their power is to teach them to mistrust their senses. This is done by insisting that the child does not see what s/he sees, or hear what she or he hears.

Examples: A child hears the mother crying, but Mother says, "No," she was laughing. A child mentions something that she or he picked up telepathically or from an aura, but the parent denies it. A child converses with a deceased grandparent and is scolded or laughed at for having a big imagination!

The apparent authority figure is undisciplined and often abusive. *The person who instigates abuse is not the perpetrator.*

Example: A mother who orders or manipulates the father into battering their child, often by lying about the child's behavior.

It is hard to see who is doing what because one person works through another, from behind the scenes, creating a grand illusion.

## Saturn the Protector

The only apparent protection you have ever had is your faith and trust in life, in yourself, and/or in your God/dess.

However, those who return to Earth, having matured to this point, <u>always</u> have some type of mission or spiritual commitment. In the end, it is that mission which is their protection. Even though life may batter these natives until they learn to set their own boundaries, there is a point beyond which mental, emotional, or physical violence against them cannot go. It is the same point, beyond which violence cannot be done to the God/dess. Literally, these are carriers of eternal life and they will consciously choose the duration of their own lives–but probably not until they get there, when they deem their mission completed.

## Personal Space and Boundaries

This can be quite difficult because, unless consciously and deliberately set, our personal space has no limits. We are like the Sun, whose edges cannot be seen behind the corona. Each of us has a type of auric corona, which flickers and fluctuates similarly to the solar corona. Thus, neither we, nor others, recognize any limits on our personal space.

Consequently, we may have to learn not to invade the space of others during our early years. Most learn rather quickly because we are naturally intelligent and observant. The obvious lesson is that we do not always know what is best for others, <u>and</u> we must learn not to help others unless asked.

Tender-hearted forgiving, during our early years, our lives are often invaded by human parasites and/or psychic vampires. The great lesson to be learned is that this happens because we have set no limits on what behavior we will accept from others. Until we learn to set some boundaries, our lives are seemingly left out in the open, in a way that invites others to help them selves to our time, energy and property.

This can go on for years, because we feel that others need us and/or that they cannot help their behavior. Still, if our lives are not to be used up by others, we must learn tough love. We must learn to let others take the consequences of their own actions or inaction. We must refuse roles that involve enabling of the incompetent.

## Setting Boundaries

Visualize or affirm a circle drawn around yourself. Make it small at first if you need to, as you must be able to believe it exists. Inside that circle is your space and you make the rules. Choose what energies and experiences you will allow inside the circle and what you want kept out.

Example: Only honest and trustworthy people can enter. This means that dishonest, untrustworthy people must change or leave. Always set the rules based on behavior, not individual people.

The size of, and rules for, your circle can change at will, according to need and your comfort zone. You will find it much easier to keep unwanted experience out of your life than to learn how to deal with it once it gets in.

## Personal Definition

Many natives enter a world in which Master Beings are believed not to exist. People cannot see what they do not believe exists. Consequently, natives may go unseen and unnamed for years. When others cannot see us, they cannot mirror us, which makes it difficult to see ourselves. We may intuitively know that we are master beings—or at least spiritually older than others—but we have difficulty accepting this as anything but imagination. The same world that discounts masters, also largely devalues imagination as the creative function that it is. Early on, we are often taught to doubt our abilities, even our very Selves.

An accurate personal definition becomes a major task in life. Meanwhile, we are left with defining ourselves against other–largely negative–examples. While others can define themselves by the people they attract in relationship, these must realize that they initially attract those who show them what they are not. When enough experience of the "I am not" is accumulated, we may conclude that what is left is what we are–the most intelligent, the most perceptive, the most creative humans on earth at any given time.

Ultimately, we are masters of the type described by our Sun's sign.

Some Examples: Aries— Master Survivor and/or one who is pioneering a new level of mastery—literally a Seed Being. Taurus—Master Builder/Creator, one who has mastered the art of attraction for creative purposes. Gemini—Master of communication and/or master of word power. Creative Consciousness. Cancer— Master of Birth and Rebirth and/or of Growth and/or of the (creative) use of feelings and emotions.

## Responsibility

The primary responsibility attached to Pisces Saturn is simply to live out our inherent mastery. This means making it conscious. It means recognizing and owning it. It means realizing and accepting that we are, in some way, set apart, anointed, called—or, that we have made a significant pre-incarnational commitment. Birth with Saturn in Pisces *always* marks a volunteer incarnation. It is granted *only* to those who have graduated from the wheel of karma. Consequently, it is and must be, our responsibility to be different from the general population. How different, or in what ways, will be suggested by the sign and house placement of natal Uranus.

## Maturity

Ours is the most mature definition possible at the time in which we incarnate. We may not be ultimate masters, but we have mastered the level of awareness for the current age—currently the age of Pisces, shortly the age of Aquarius. Consequently our lives are intended as living lessons for all the people in them.

The general belief that maturity means consistency, staying focused on a goal, or playing specific, historically-defined roles is meaningless for Pisces Saturn. For us, true maturity consists of realizing that we are born ahead of our times and that we must learn to live somewhat in advance of those around us. We cannot, and must not try, to fit-in. We are the leaders for our times, showing the way to higher levels of awareness and being.

Maturity means following our own inner leading, ignoring most of the rules—either laws or those beliefs about the way life works—and living a totally uncontained lifestyle.

## Authority and Rights

We are authorized to live out the master's way. We have the right to determine methods and morality for ourselves. We are agents of Spirit, authorized representatives of Divine Will on Earth at any given time. In one sense or another, each is a guru, priest/tess or prophet. As such, we have the right to Divine protection and supply. When Jesus ben Joseph said, "Take my yoke upon you . . . for my yoke is easy and my burden is light," it was in reference to us. Translated to modern language the command might be, "You take care of your mission, calling or commitment, and let me take care of you." For most, much of materiality is literally none of our business!

## Saturn's Law

This is the Law of Mastery, rather like a Doctorate in Humanity. It is the promise that our ultimate incarnational intent is to earn a PhD in consciousness. This opportunity is open to all, but it takes lifetimes to complete. When we are born with Saturn in Pisces we can be certain that we have many lifetimes behind us.

PhD degrees are always earned, although not always in the same way. Some are the result of formal schooling and some are awarded in recognition of life experience. Saturn in Pisces can be regarded as an award given for accumulation of both education and experience. It refers to the shape which a particular incarnation takes. That shape is the living outline of human potential.

---

[20]There are levels of mastery related to phases of human evolution.

# Appendix: Keywords for Saturn

Limits: A limit is like a leash or tether. It is the measure of, or inhibiting factor that defines our range of motion, activity, or travel. In a natal horoscope, by sign, Saturn describes our personal limits. Its house describes their most active area.

Boundaries: A boundary fixes the parameters or scope of a person, place, or thing. Boundaries include outlines, borders, edges, fences, walls, property lines, and human skin. Natal Saturn describes our personal space, indicating the location and nature of our personal boundaries.

Definitions: A definition is a boundary of meaning around an idea or concept. Definitions may include descriptions of appearance, activity, potential, and antithesis. A thing is this and not that. The human skeleton is included in this area, because it defines the height and shape of our body.

Discipline: Discipline is about learning, or teaching the recognition and consideration of consequences. (Noun) A discipline is a set of behaviors, usually conditioned by a belief system—as a spiritual discipline which might require regular performance of certain rituals. (Verb) To discipline is to set and enforce boundaries for another. It is the function of authority figures to determine the consequences of transgressing those boundaries.

Self-Discipline: This is about setting our own limits and managing our lives rationally. *Abuse is not discipline.* Children cannot learn self-discipline from an undisciplined adult.

Authority: Authority is the right or power to give commands, enforce obedience, take action or make final decisions. Three types of authority are: Delegated, as the legal system, police, judges, and earned, the result of attaining knowledge or experience, as professionals, teachers, gurus, and automatic, the authority over children of parents and other adult authority figures.

Authority Figure: In a natal chart, Saturn represents the Authority Figure, describing the final authority in our birth family, the person who sets boundaries and is responsible for discipline, also the family business manager.

Responsibility: Literally, the ability to respond, as responsive. Today it is usually used to mean the acceptance of an obligation, accountability and/or the care and discipline of another or others. *We are morally responsible only for ourselves and our minor children.* We also have some limited responsibility for all naturally dependant beings—other people's children, domestic plants, animals.

Maturity: To have crossed sufficient age boundaries–physical, mental, emotional, spiritual–to have achieved self-awareness, self-discipline and/or self-control. The achievement of a level of authority and the rights that accompany it.

Adulthood, Elders, Elderly: all words assigned to Saturn on the assumption that they have reached maturity.

Rights: With every responsibility, with every new level of maturity, come certain rights and rewards: This is the great over-looked face of Saturn. With maturity, we are authorized to have and do certain things.

www.ingramcontent.com/pod-product-compliance
Lightning Source LLC
Chambersburg PA
CBHW080539090426

42733CB00016B/2633